GAZING ON THE PAST

GAZING ON THE PAST

A Study on History and Historiography

Lalfakawma Ralte

Christian World Imprints

First Published in 2024 by

Christian World Imprints
Christian Publishing & Books from India
A-71 Group, Wazirpur Industrial Area
Delhi-110052
cwidelhi2017@gmail.com
www.ChristianWorldImprints.com
Phone: +91 11 41526079

ISBN: 978-93-6065-941-7 (HB)
ISBN: 978-93-6065-913-4 (PB)

Printed in India.

Contents

Acknowledgement

I would like to express my sincere gratitude to my colleagues at United Theological College (U.T.C.) in Bangalore and Aizawl Theological College (A.T.C.) in Aizawl for their invaluable support and collaboration throughout my academic journey. Special thanks are due to Professor Rev. Vanlalchhuanawma, my esteemed teacher and colleague at A.T.C. I owe a great deal to him for enriching my perspective in the field of historical studies. Under his mentorship, I gained a deeper understanding of historical research and critical thinking skills. He encouraged me to approach and interpret historical narratives that are often overlooked by mainstream historians.

I am profoundly grateful to Professor Rev. H. Lalrinthanga, who provided valuable guidance and support during my time at A.T.C. His commitment to excellence and his genuine care for my academic and personal growth have been instrumental in shaping my journey.

Professor Rev. V. V. Thomas, my guide during my doctoral studies and now my admired colleague at U.T.C., has been a beacon of knowledge and inspiration for me. His profound insights and unwavering support have shaped my understanding of history and enriched my perspective on life. He encouraged me to explore new dimensions of history, particularly the neglected narratives of subaltern and other subjugated communities.

Dr. Kaholi Zhimomi, my esteemed colleague at U.T.C., has been a constant source of inspiration for me. Her dedication to her field and her commitment to fostering excellence in historical scholarship are truly commendable. Her vision of cultivating a new generation of Indian historians is truly admirable and inspiring. Working alongside Dr. Kaholi has been a privilege for me, as her enthusiasm and expertise enrich our academic community at United Theological College. Her insights and commitment to her students and colleagues alike are invaluable, and I am grateful for the guidance and support she provides.

I am deeply indebted to my wife, Mathani, and our four daughters, Ainam, Zualtei, Felfeli, and Faith. Their unwavering support and understanding have been instrumental in my academic pursuits. Their selflessness in relieving me of household chores, encouragement, and the nurturing environment they provide at home have been invaluable to my writing journey. Mathani's tireless efforts and sacrifices enable me to focus on my research and writing even during moments of idleness or discouragement. Her belief in me and her willingness to shoulder the responsibilities of daily life has been a constant source of strength. I am also grateful to our daughters for their support and understanding, which have enabled me to pursue my academic goals with greater confidence and determination. To my beloved family, I express my gratitude for being my pillars of strength and for your unwavering belief in my work. Your sacrifices and encouragement mean more to me than words can express.

This book is a result of my passion for historical inquiry, which is guided by God's divine providence. As the source of all wisdom and inspiration, God has been with me throughout my academic journey, giving me the courage to persevere through moments of uncertainty and doubt. I acknowledge God's divine presence and guidance, which have been with me every step of the way. As the Beginning and the End of history, God's providence has shaped the course of the events of humanity and continues to illuminate the path of my research and writing. It is through God's grace that I can delve into the complexities of the past and share its lessons with others. I dedicate this book to the glory of God, who reigns supreme over all of history.

Dear readers, I extend my warmest appreciation for your interest in delving into the world of history with me. Your curiosity and eagerness to explore the past are truly commendable. As you embark on this journey, I am grateful for your willingness to engage with the ideas and narratives presented within these pages. It is my sincere hope that you will find this book both enlightening and enjoyable. May the insights contained herein captivate your imagination and deepen your understanding of the rich tapestry of the history of human beings. I wish you a fulfilling and enlightening reading experience.

Happy reading!

Warm regards,

Lalfakawma Ralte
UTC, Bangalore, 2024

Preface

Welcome to an exploration of history – a journey through time, philosophy, and the depths of the experience of human beings. This book is a testament to the enduring relevance and complexity of history, designed to enrich the minds of college students, whether they attend theological institutions or secular campuses. *Gazing on the Past (A Study on History and Historiography)* delves into the multifaceted nature of history, unravelling its meaning, philosophy, and various approaches.

From the study of historiography to the critical examination of historical writing, this book offers a comprehensive toolkit for those with a passion for historical inquiry. History, as we will discover, is not merely a recollection of events; it reflects human identity, aspirations, and struggles. It is the lens through which we make sense of the past, confront the present, and shape the future. Throughout these pages, we will navigate through the nuances of historical interpretation, exploring how different perspectives can shed light on the same events.

One of the central themes of this book is the use and misuse of history. We will uncover how historical narratives can be weaponized for political, cultural, or ideological agendas, and how discernment is essential in evaluating historical sources and claims. In a world inundated with information, understanding the complexities of historical analysis is more crucial than ever.

For students of the Senate of Serampore College and Asia Theological Association, this book serves as a guide through the intricacies of historical scholarship. However, its reach extends beyond theological realms, offering valuable insights to all those who seek to deepen their understanding of the past.

To the students, learners, and teachers who embark on this journey, I present this book as a companion in your pursuit of historical knowledge. May it inspire you to engage critically with the past, question assumptions, and appreciate the richness of the experience of humanity within the annals of history.

As we venture into the realm of historical inquiry, let us remember the words of the historian Marc Bloch: "The historian is, by definition, absolutely incapable of observing the past as it happened." With this humility and awareness, let us embark on this intellectual voyage together.

Sincerely,

Lalfakawma Ralte
United Theological College
Bangalore

Chapter 1

What is History?

1. What is History?

1.1. Definitions

It is generally accepted that the ancient Greeks were the earliest to define history.[1] As one of the earliest historians in the Western tradition, Herodotus was a Greek historian who lived in the 5th century B.C.E. He is frequently referred to as the "father of history."[2] He contributed to laying the groundwork for contemporary research into historical events and societies.

The word history comes from the Greek word *ἱστορία* (*historía*), meaning inquiry, the act of seeking knowledge, as well as the knowledge that results from inquiry. It means that history is the knowledge acquired by investigation. It is the systematic study and documentation of a human being's past. In other words, history is a record of events. It refers to all-time

---

[1] See Neville Morley, *Writing Ancient History* (New Delhi: Bloomsbury, 1999), 24. Hereafter cited as Morley, *Writing Ancient History.*

[2] See Sotirios Majoros, *All About Me: The Individual* (Victoria, Canada: Friesen Press, 2019), 10.

preceding this very moment and everything that happened up to now.[3] It is a form of discourse about the past.

For Geoffrey Barraclough, history is "the attempt to discover based on fragmentary evidence the significant thing about the past."[4] When we discuss history as a social need, we are talking about the history that we are concerned with. It has to do with research and discoveries. Some investigations are undoubtedly more fruitful than others: in some eras, topics that we now consider to be mere superstition, myth, or polemic were important.[5]

For Aristotle, history is an account of the unchanging past. For him, the past, by its very nature, can never change. According to this, history is the explanation of human achievements where there would be no room for isolated facts or events. In a broader sense, history is a way to explain the present by referring to the stages it has gone through. In the words of G. I. Renier, history is "the memories of societies."[6] Collective memory, the shared repository of knowledge that a group of people holds about their past, is another name for the memories of civilizations. People can retain information from the past and use it to make sense of the present. A society's identity, culture, and behaviour can all be influenced by collective memory.

Let us observe the following examples of communal memory. How different countries recollect and celebrate historic occurrences like battles, revolutions, or natural calamities is one example. Another instance is how successive generations have distinct viewpoints and feelings on the same events. A fundamental aspect of a nation's identity and viewpoint can be understood by understanding their recollections. "Countries do

---

[3] Katy Steinmetz, "This is Where the Word History Comes From," History Word Origin: What Is History and Where Term Is From | Time (12 July 2023).

[4] Geoffrey Barraclough, *History in a Changing World* (England: Oxford Blackwell, 1955), 15.

[5] See Arthur Marwick, *The Nature of History* (London: Macmillan, 1970), 15.

[6] Henry L. Roediger, III, K. Andrew DeSoto, "The Power of Collective Memory," https://www.scientificamerican.com/article/the-power-of-collective-memory/ (18 July 2023). Hereafter cited as Roediger, "The Power."

not have memories;"[7] instead, the citizens are the ones who keep their memories alive.

The term "collective memory" refers to the collective memory of a group. Citizens in India recall their country's freedom from the British, while the Chinese people recall the Cultural Revolution and the events that followed. Moreover, more regional levels of collective memory may also exist. Families may recall their past or a certain important day. Any significant social group to which we belong has some type of collective memory for each of us.[8] These accumulated memories may contain facts or interpretations.

Webster's categorization of definitions of history into three clusters - "thought, record or events"[9] is a thing to really mull over. Some individuals think of history as a function of human perception. They view history as nostalgia and recollections of the past. Others view history as principally being a record of the past. And last, some people see history as happenings[10] or goings-on.

According to David C. McCullough, history serves as a link that joins the past and present.[11] History is the study of the past. It contains all the historical records that may be read and examined now. McCullough makes a bridge analogy here. History links the past and the present in a similar way to how a bridge connects two locations. By studying history, people in the present can learn about the past. The different sides of history - history as a record and history as a human reflection on that record - present the link.

The present shapes how we perceive the past. Some have even argued that believing what the historical records claim happened is the closest thing we can come to knowing what actually happened. Since historical knowledge is based on what

---

[7] Roediger, "The Power," 2.

[8] See Roediger, "The Power," 3.

[9] John C. B. Webster, *An Introduction to History*, 2nd ed. (Delhi: Macmillan, 1981), 14. Hereafter cited as Webster, *An Introduction.*

[10] See Webster, *An Introduction*, 14.

[11] As cited by Maartje Abbenhuis, "The Present as History," The Present as History - Fifteen Eightyfour | Cambridge University Press (cambridgeblog.org) (14 July 2023).

has been believed about the past, all history is, therefore, "the history of thought,"[12] as Webster agreeably puts it.

Gazing at the history of the "past" which has gone with the wind for many could be mind-numbing, wearisome, and boring. For them, history has limited and negative connotations. Durant asserts, "Most history is guessing, and the rest is prejudice,"[13] Such reluctance echoes A. J. Toynbee's *ipse dixit* that history is just one damned thing after another.[14] The past, for Collingwood, too is a "dead" past, which is a rigid and irreversible collection of data.[15] Whereas the history of what went before may be perceived by some as dead, dull, and dreary, it is fascinating on another hand to know that it (history) is an ever-changing account of the unchanging past. History is the lively, vibrant, dynamic, and ever-growing subject which inflamed E. H. Carr to remark that it "is a continuous process of interaction between the historian and his [sic] facts, an unending dialogue between the present and the past."[16] The dynamic of change in conversation with the past, recording events that have gone by and elucidation of what went before is a never-ending affair which a serious historian cannot afford to overlook.

1.2. Nature and Scope of History

Previously, history was commonly perceived as a mere chronicle of events presented descriptively. Those who recorded these accounts were identified as chroniclers, distinct from historians. However, we now comprehend that the historian's role extends beyond that of a chronicler, as history encompasses much more than a simple chronicle of events. It is therefore essential to note that the historian's task is not limited to providing a chronological account

---

[12] Webster, *An Introduction*, 28.

[13] Will and Ariel Durant, *The Lessons of History* (Bombay: Mohan Pajabi Hans Publishers, 1968), 7. Hereafter cited as Durant, *The Lessons.*

[14] "History is Just One Damn Thing after Another," https://quoteinvestigator.com/2015/09/16/history/ (10 Aug. 2018).

[15] For detailed elaboration see Paul Q. Hirst, *Marxism and Historical Writing* (New York: Routledge, 2017), 43.

[16] E. H. Carr, *What is History?* reprinted (Harmondsworth, Middlesex, England, Penguin Books Ltd, 1981), 30. Hereafter cited as Carr, *What is History?*

of past events, but also to interpreting and imbuing them with meaning for contemporary audiences. In this way, history becomes a continuous interaction between the past and the present. To this end, it is necessary to analyze historical events thoroughly and objectively. The historian's role is to objectively understand the past to comprehend the present, rather than to glorify or detach from the past. The historian's interpretation of the past should be based on logical and critical analysis, free from personal biases and prejudices. Therefore, the historian's task is not simply to describe past events, but also to explain their relevance and significance to the present. Simply put, the historian's role is to bridge the divide between the past and the present by interpreting historical events objectively and with meaning. By doing so, historians enable us to learn from the past and make well-informed decisions for the future.

1.2.1. Nature of History

1.2.1.1. History is a Special Form of Thought

History is a unique way of thinking. As a result, people with two qualifications should be able to answer questions about the nature, object, method, and importance of this type of mental activity. Firstly, they must have previous experience with this type of thinking. They must be experts in history. It is essential to look at supposed facts with a fresh perspective. It is necessary to question whether widely accepted truths are accurate or false. Secondly, individuals must have not only experienced historical thinking but also reflected on it.[17] They must be both historians and philosophers, with a specific focus on historical concepts and challenges.

1.2.1.2. History Repeats Itself

The idea of history repeating itself has sparked a lot of discussion among historians over the years. While some scholars posit that certain events and patterns recur throughout

---

[17] See R. G. Collingwood, *The Idea of History*, revised ed. (New York: Oxford University Press, 2007), 7, 8.

history, others dismiss this notion as mere coincidence.[18] This issue has sparked significant debates about the cyclical nature of history and what insights we may learn from analysing the past. The overarching idea of cyclical theory is derived from the phenomenon of persistent historical events. Meanwhile, Christian historians believe in the linear theory, which holds that history progresses from the past to the future. They agree that historical events are continuous and have a connection between the past and the present. This constant flow influences the linear nature of history. This movement is seen as one of development and growth. Even Carr seemed to believe in the linear conception of history, stating, "The belief that we have come from somewhere is closely linked with the belief that we are going somewhere."[19]

Concerning this, scholars should mull over the following aspects:

What about those who believe that events appear cyclical merely because human beings repeat similar errors again and again? Have you considered the opposite opinion that history is neither cyclical nor linear, but rather entirely unexpected and chaotic? How would you respond to someone who claims that the notion of cycle theory is out of date and no longer applicable to contemporary times?

1.2.1.3. History Deals with How People Have Lived Throughout Time

Throughout time, people have lived through various experiences that have shaped the course of human history. History is the study of events that have occurred at specific points in time, and it provides us with a unique perspective on the evolution of humanity. The story of humanity is one of continuous development, and time adds a certain charm that enhances the past. The study of history is inextricably linked to the story of humanity, as it reveals the threads

---

[18] See K. L. Khurana, *Concepts and Methods of Historiography*, 8th edition (Agra: Lakshmi Narayan Agarwal, 2017), 5. Hereafter cited as Khurana, *Concepts*.

[19] Carr, *What is History?* 132.

of human life, the challenges we have faced, the victories we have achieved, and the cultural progress we have made. As we look back on the past, we are reminded that before us, other human beings roamed the earth. Species such as Ardipithecus, Australopithecus, and numerous homo species have lived on our planet for millions of years, each leaving their mark on the course of human history. Humanity even coexisted alongside the Neanderthals for some time,[20] a fascinating fact that reminds us of our shared past and the rich tapestry of human history.

Here, a historian must be alert to respond to someone who believes that history is irrelevant to our current lives and that we should focus solely on the present and future. He/she must consider the argument that studying history often perpetuates a Eurocentric or Western-centric perspective, neglecting the experiences and contributions of non-Western cultures. He/she must be able to answer those who argue that history is written by the victors and therefore, cannot be trusted as an accurate representation of the past.

1.2.1.4. Unending Dialogue

E. H. Carr, a renowned historian, believed that the true value of a historian lies not in merely recording past events, but in their ability to clarify and settle as many disputes or controversies regarding the past as possible. In other words, a historian's role is not limited to presenting a factual account of historical events, but rather to interpreting and providing a deeper understanding of the past, to resolve any conflicting interpretations or perspectives about it. This unending dialogue between historians and their audience not only helps to enrich our knowledge of history but also brings us closer to a more accurate and nuanced understanding of our collective past.

A historian must consider the following questions. What about the likelihood that historical reports are impacted by the historian's prejudices and perspectives, and thus are not entirely objective? Have you examined the constraint of historical evidence

---

[20] See Russell Howard Tuttle, "Human Evolution," https://www.britannica.com/science/human-evolution (13 Apr. 2024).

and how this affects the historian's capacity to present a thorough and accurate assessment of previous events? How would you respond to people who believe that there is no way to completely resolve historical disagreements since what we know of the past is constantly growing and subject to change?

1.2.1.5. Variation in History

The study of history is a complex and multifaceted endeavour. Historical accounts vary not only across different times but also among historians. That is because the interpretation of historical events is shaped by the prevailing ideas, beliefs, and values of the era in which the historian lives.[21] The historian's perception of the past is influenced by their experiences, cultural background, and political views. For instance, the history written during the colonial period often reflects the biases and prejudices of the colonizers, while the history produced after independence may offer a more balanced and nuanced perspective. Therefore, to truly understand history, we must examine it from multiple perspectives and consider the context in which it was produced.

1.2.1.6. Interpretation of History

Historical inquiry is an important aspect of understanding the past. Historians often use accessible facts to develop accounts of past events. However, the interpretation of these events is subjective and heavily influenced by the historian's standpoint, prejudices, and the social and cultural context in which they work. Therefore, history is characterized by a range of interpretations, which encourages ongoing discourse and debate among researchers. Serious historians do not just recount events, but also investigate the connections between them. They analyse and compare different historical events to develop general laws. These laws are then tested through comparison with similar events in different communities to increase their trustworthiness and legitimacy. This process of investigation and comparison

[21] See Khurana, *Concepts*, 7.

help historians to understand the past better and provide a more accurate account of historical events.

Historians must consider important questions while conducting their research. For instance, should they apply universal laws to individual events, even if they oversimplify complicated historical phenomena? They also need to be aware of their own biases, which can lead to the omission of essential information and perspectives. Furthermore, some people argue that multiple interpretations of historical events can result in a lack of common ground, ultimately undermining the credibility of historical investigation. How would you respond to such a claim?

1.2.1.7. Evolution of History

Over time, the study of history has undergone significant changes, reflecting advancements in techniques, hypotheses, and historiographical tendencies. The discipline of history is continually evolving and diversifying, moving beyond conventional methods that focus primarily on political elites and key events. Today, there is a growing emphasis on more inclusive and multidisciplinary frameworks that consider the perspectives of marginalized groups and cultural dynamics.

The evolution of history as a discipline can be traced back to the late 19th and early 20th centuries. During this period, historians began to question the traditional approach to history, which largely ignored the experiences of ordinary people and focused on the deeds of great people. Instead, they sought to uncover the social, economic, and cultural forces that shaped historical events. This shift towards a more inclusive approach to history gained momentum in the latter half of the 20th century. Historians began to explore the experiences of marginalized groups such as women, people of colour, and the working class, shedding light on aspects of history that had previously been overlooked.

This approach also led to the development of new fields of study, such as social history, cultural history, and gender history. Today, the study of history continues to evolve and diversify. Historians are increasingly using multidisciplinary approaches that draw on insights from fields such as anthropology, sociology, and literary studies. This approach allows for a more nuanced understanding of historical events, as well as a greater appreciation for the diversity of human experience.

1.2.2. Scope of History

The academic discipline of history is characterised by its extensive range, encompassing topics that span from ancient times to the present day. Its reach extends across time, space, and fields of inquiry, revealing the interplay of human societies and their interactions with the natural world. Through its multidisciplinary approach, history sheds light on the complex relationships between cultures, highlighting how they have developed and evolved.

1.2.2.1. Widening Scope

Historians have come a long way in their approach to the past. In the past, the focus of historical narratives was on the leaders and rulers, such as kings and church leaders. However, today's historians take a much more critical mindset and strive to give prominence to people on the periphery. This approach has contributed to the popularity of microhistory writing, which delves into the lives and experiences of individuals whom historians may have overlooked in broader narratives.

Today's historical research emphasises women even though early writers overlooked them.[22] This shift in focus has brought about a broader perspective on history, recognizing the contributions and experiences of all members of society. Furthermore, history has moved beyond being a mere subset of literary work, politics, philosophy, or any other discipline. It now stands independently as a field of study, with its primary function being society's developing culture. That includes expertise, belief, artistic endeavours, ethical behaviour, habits, and additional talents or customs gained by humanity as an integral part of a community. Today, history scholars accept that their primary tasks are data collection and interpretation. Historians aim to describe what took place, examine how it unfolded, and assess the reasons

---

[22] See Khurana, *Concepts*, 7, 8.

for its occurrence.[23] Through these tasks, history serves as a critical tool for understanding the past and informing our decisions in the present and future.

1.2.2.2. History Encompasses All of Humanity's Endeavours

The specialist in history must look outside governance to citizens, beyond ordinances to mythology, beyond theology to mythology and cultural heritage, and he or she should investigate any occurrence that has a psychological, economic, theoretical, subject matter, ethical, or psychological significance to human beings in society.[24] History should contain all facets of human achievement, including technological, and scientific discoveries, and experiences. History largely focuses on human social life, political successes, cultural accomplishments, institutional oversight, and economic ambitions, as state and society shape humanity's uniqueness.

1.2.2.3. From Objective Experimentation to Historicism

History, as a discipline, has come a long way from merely presenting objective facts to include historicism. Objective experimentation, or the traditional way of studying history, focuses on facts as they exactly happened, without any bias or interpretation. It aimed to provide a replica of how things were in the past based on concrete evidence. However, this method was criticized for being incomplete and limited, as it failed to capture the complexity of historical events. On the other hand, historicism is a more nuanced approach to studying history that considers the growth and development of an event or phenomenon from its inception. It views history as a dynamic process that evolves and changes over time, like a biological process. This method takes the various factors that influence the development of an event, such as social, political, economic, and cultural factors, among others. It also considers the role of human agency in shaping historical

[23] See Paominlen Kipgen, "Historiography, Definitions, Nature and Scope of History," https://www.academia.edu/31041228/Historiography_Definitions_Nature_and_Scope_of_History (16 Apr. 2024). Hereafter cited as Kipgen, "Historiography."

[24] See Kipgen, "Historiography," 1.

events and the impact of external forces that may have affected the outcome.[25] In essence, historicism provides a more complete and comprehensive understanding of history, as it goes beyond just presenting objective facts to analysing the process of historical change and development. It recognises that history is not just a collection of isolated events, but a continuous narrative shaped by various factors and influences.

1.2.2.4. Material Scope

History's material and worldly scope includes all human existence, from prehistoric periods to the present. Historians examine distinct times, phases, and ages to identify recurring trends in stability and shifts over time. The secular or temporal perspective of history enables historians to contextualise events, movements, and changes within larger historical narratives, shedding light on the rise and fall of civilisations and communities.

1.3. Philosophies of History

In the eighteenth century, Voltaire, a great French philosopher used the term philosophy of history. Philosophy of history is the philosophical study of history and its discipline. The term was coined by the French philosopher Voltaire. He was a French philosopher who criticized the established notions of history and reinterpreted the moral, aesthetic, and religious views of ancient civilizations.[12] He was considered to be the first person to coin the term "philosophy of history" and to study history based on culture. To Voltaire 'philosophy of history' is a critical or scientific history in which the historian thinks for himself/herself, instead of repeating the stories[26] contained in earlier works.

There are speculative philosophy and critical philosophy of history. While speculative philosophy is formal and material, critical philosophy is analytical and synoptic. Critical philosophy deals with the philosophical analysis of historiography and inquiries

---

[25] See Kipgen, "Historiography," 1.

[26] See H. Gowri Naidu, *Philosophy of History*, JETIR, 1/6, November 2014: 1560-1572. Hereafter cited as Naidu, *Philosophy of History.*

into the logical, conceptual, and epistemological characterization of what historians do. Speculative philosophy attempts to discover some meaning or significance in concepts which transcend the intelligibility achieved by ordinary historical works.

1.3.1. Speculative Philosophy of History

Speculative Philosophy is formal and empirical. It tries to unearth some significance or meaning in ideas that go above the level of comprehension attained by conventional historical works. It stands for the desire to understand the processes of growth and decay and the search for unity among the events' confusing complexity.[27] Speculative philosophy views that throughout human history, there has been a visible, larger scheme or design, some overarching goal or pattern.

Plato and Aristotle, who developed their views about the structure of government, are considered the fathers of the speculative philosophy of history. The theories advanced by speculative philosophy do not follow any predefined patterns. There are two categories within it: the teleological speculative system and the scientific speculative system.

1.3.2. Teleological Speculative System

This system aims to demonstrate that historical events had some sort of plan or purpose. This was a longstanding, established idea. For Christians, history is like a play in a theatre with a predetermined beginning and finale. Several Christian authors from the fifth century, with St. Augustine, to the seventeenth century held the providentially predetermined plan to be true. Empires and cultures were supposed to rise and perish because of supernatural intervention. According to a concept by which historical data are focused and brought together to form a single meaning, the Christian approach aimed to explain history in terms of this principle. For Christians, God is active in history. Christians hold that all historical events are chaotic and that only

[27] See Naidu, *Philosophy of History*, 1570.

human beings' surrender to God's will can bring them into order.[28] Therefore, God's grace and will serve as the driving force behind historical events.

But in current times, this theory has been brutally repressed. Its worst critic was Proudhon,[29] a French philosopher. Despite being a theologian, he developed the philosophy of progress. He believes that society is driven by irrational emotions. The ability to recognise death as a social instinct belongs to human beings. Human intelligence, talent, and initiative are crucial in the ongoing conflict between human beings and nature because they help to shape the course of human history. Therefore, he contends that divine will is irrelevant to this conflict. So, Proudhon opposes God. He held that social change was a dialectical process, driven by tensions and contradictions between various social forces, rather than a linear or predetermined one. He also opposed the notion that there could ever be a final or ideal state of society and argued that federalism, mutualism, and self-government were the best ways to continuously better the lot of people.[30] Although they were not against God, Voltaire and Condorcet were equally anti-church. Voltaire had the view that if God did not exist, God would have to be created.[31] Consequently, the theological interpretation of history came under harsh criticism.

1.3.3. Scientific Approach

The term "scientific approach/theorist" refers to individuals who rejected theological interpretations of history and built their views on empirical data. The first of them were the Greeks, who tried to rationalise human behaviour. They held that historical events occurred in cycles. A key component of Plato's idea of a just city was the philosopher king. He did not specifically employ

---

[28] See Naidu, *Philosophy of History,* 1570, 1571.

[29] W. Harbold, "Progressive Humanity: In the Philosophy of P. J. Proudhon," *The Review of Politics,* 31/1: 28-47. Hereafter cited as Harbold, "Progressive Humanity."

[30] See Harbold, "Progressive Humanity," 30.

[31] See Naidu, *Philosophy of History,* 1570.

the idea of kingship; instead, he contrasted it with other systems of government like tyranny, aristocracy, and democracy. He maintained that only a king endowed with perfect wisdom and virtue could guarantee the happiness of all his subjects.[32] This eternal cyclical method was one that Aristotle also supported. The Greeks had a strong belief in the study of events as truths that were logically and permanently connected to one another.

The idea of a constant reality was central to the ancient Indian mind's working theories. There are references to a cyclical idea of creation and destruction in the *Puranas*, but they do not go as far as the church's teleological perspective. The concept of the *yugas* occurring in a set order, one after the other, was developed. Hindus traditionally divide the historical process into four phases: *Krita, Treta, Dwapara,* and *Kali*. In the first, *dharma* or virtue is paramount; in the second, it starts to wane; in the third, it starts to become rare; and in the fourth, it completely vanishes.[33] This cyclical view of history permeates Indian thinking.

The cyclical notion is also supported by the Chinese view of history. The shifting of order and disorder is how the Chinese view historical change. They held a belief in the black, white, and red cycle three sequences.[34] Their thinking is likewise predicated on the notion that the current era is one of decline. This is the central tenet of Chinese Buddhism, Taoism, and Confucianism. They always thought the past was better than the present.

Since the 17th century, speculative philosophy has advanced significantly. Hobbs favoured the idea of looking into human matters using the same methods used in natural sciences. Such a possibility signalled the beginning of a time filled with enormous hope for many enlightened historians. Vico, Kant, Condorcet,

---

[32] See Melissa Lane, "Philosopher king," Encyclopedia Britannica, 28 Feb. 2023, https://www.britannica.com/topic/philosopher-king (5 Sep. 2023).

[33] See Naidu, *Philosophy of History,* 1570, 1571.

[34] Steve Hullfish, "Psychology of Color: Does a specific color indicate a specific emotion?" http://provideocoalition.com/shullfish/story/psychology_of_color (6 Sep. 2023).

Herder, Fichte, and Hegel made significant contributions[35] in this area in the 18th century.

Numerous speculative hypotheses were in fashion in the 19th century. They are theories that come from idealism, materialism, biology, and romanticism. Spengler, Sorokin, and Toynbee significantly expanded on the topic in the 20th century. The prevailing school of thinking holds that if physical nature produces laws with universal applicability, history, which makes up just a small portion of natural activity, may likewise be reduced to laws. The Italian philosopher Giambattista Vico believed that history moves in cycles. Societies organically grow and then deteriorate according to his cyclical theory of history, known as *Corsi e Ricorsi,* i.e., cycles and counter cycles of history.[36] He proposed the existence of a bestial condition, a period of the gods, and a time of heroes, all of which result in oligarchies, or the rule of the richest. After that, there is a male-dominated era marked by class tension, which lasts until society falls apart. Vico used this hypothesis to explain the development of Rome,[37] from its mythical founders Romulus and Remus to the barbarian invasions that led to its downfall.

History was characterised by Kant and Condeceret as the development of human reason. Herder views history as the cyclical progression of the emergence, development, deterioration, and demise of all life forms. Hegel created the most audacious metaphysical analysis of historical processes. The theme of history, according to him, is the realisation of the absolute in time and the self-development of the spirit via the lives and times of many historical figures from around the world. In the 19th century, Auguste Compte served as the positivist movement's prophet.[38] According to

---

[35] See Naidu, *Philosophy of History,* 1572.

[36] See http://hispanoteca.eu/Foro/ARCHIVO-Foro/Corsi%20e%20ricorsi.htm (13 Sep. 2023).

[37] "What was Vico's cyclical idea of history?" ebrary.net/5101/philosophy/vicos_cyclical_idea_history (ebrary.net) (6 Sep. 2023).

[38] See "Auguste Comte Positivism," www.studyandexam.com/comte-positivism.html (6 Sep. 2023).

him, no reality could be philosophically grasped without first being understood historically.[39]

1.3.4. Critical/Analytical Philosophy of History

At the end of the 19th century, philosophers started to become interested in the task of attempting to define the distinctive character of historical knowledge and understanding rather than in the older method of attempting to develop huge speculative frameworks. The idea that history might be viewed as nothing more than a meaningless mess in the absence of some all-encompassing teleological or quasi-scientific structure was completely unacceptable to intellectuals like Wilhelm Dilthey and Benedetto Croce. They held that history is comprehensible in the sense that historians make it so.[40] Furthermore, they thought that this was the only kind of comprehensibility that was either required or appropriate to demand.

What could be fairly sought after was a clearer and deeper understanding of the circumstances that make historical knowledge feasible, as well as an explanation of the underlying assumptions and guiding principles that guide historical inquiry. The British philosopher R. G. Collingwood, who was heavily influenced by Crocean's thought, stated in his Autobiography (1939) that "the chief business of twentieth-century philosophy is to reckon with twentieth-century history."[41]

Collingwood and his continental predecessors effectively contributed significantly to reorienting the philosophy of history by arguing that the philosopher should focus on articulating and justifying current historical practises rather than attempting to provide a splendid overview of the entire historical process. The widespread acceptance of analytical methodologies in other disciplines of philosophy also provided additional support for

[39] See Naidu, *Philosophy of History*, 1572.

[40] See Patrick Lancaster Gardiner, "Analytical Problems, the Concept of History," https://www.britannica.com/contributor/Patrick-Lancaster-Gardiner/1025 (13 Sep. 2023). Hereafter cited as Gardiner, "Analytical Problems."

[41] See Gardiner, "Analytical Problems," 5.

their views. Therefore, later thinkers tended to concentrate on the definition of terms and concepts that are crucial to historical thought and description as these are actually carried out.[42] This led them to discuss topics like how historians typically divide up and categorise the past, how they defend and support their interpretations, and the logical structure of the explanations they are used to providing.

1.4. Uses and Abuses of History

Understanding history is crucial to understanding how past events have shaped the present. However, it is common for people to misuse and abuse history, leading to significant impacts on politics, society, and culture. This topic explores the complex relationship between the use and misuse of history, highlighting its various manifestations and effects. Historical events can be interpreted in different ways, such as being used to establish power, justify legal claims, or legitimize control over the present. National histories often intersect or overlap with one another, leading to conflicts between official history and collective memory.[43] By studying both the use and abuse of history, we can gain insight into these issues.

1.4.1. Uses of History

1.4.1.1. It Promotes Self-understanding

Historical knowledge is an essential aspect of everyday studying, as it provides critical information for interpreting familiar references, such as people, locations, dates, and events. By understanding the concepts and records of the past, we develop a better awareness of ourselves[44] and our surroundings.

However, it is important to note that historical knowledge can vary from the self-understanding of the individuals who created the records and concepts. Despite this, historical interpretation

---

[42] See Gardiner, "Analytical Problems," 7.

[43] See Marc Ferro, *The Use and Abuse of History* (London, New York: Routledge, 2012) Preface, x.

[44] See Laxmi Jain, *Historical Method and Historiography* (New Delhi: Vayu Education of India, 2016), 7. Hereafter cited as Jain, *Historical Method.*

must analyze and comprehend that distinct self-understanding as a critical component of reconstructing the past. These two aspects of historical cognition are vital for recreating the past, whether for a precise depiction of the past in and of itself or for the use of the past's records for our contemporary context. Historical knowledge helps us to understand our cultural heritage, social norms, and how our society evolved.[45] By examining the events and circumstances of the past, we can gain valuable insights into how to navigate the complexities of our modern world. In essence, historical knowledge is a crucial tool for anyone seeking to better understand themselves and the world around them.

Historians must be prepared to respond to critical questions. For instance, how should one approach someone who thinks that comprehending modern society does not require knowledge of history? Is it possible that the biases and perspectives of the interpreters could influence historical cognition? Additionally, what about those who claim that the reconstruction of the past is impossible due to the subjectivity of historical interpretation?

1.4.1.2. It Gives Proper Conception of Time, Space, and Society

The study of history is crucial to gaining a comprehensive understanding of the world around us. It provides us with the tools to comprehend the concepts of time, space, and society, and to recognize the interconnectivity between these three elements. By examining the past, we gain insights into the present, enabling us to make more informed decisions about our future. Moreover, history helps us to understand our place in the world and our relationship with those who came before us. It serves as a link between individuals and the larger communities to which we belong.[46] By examining the events and experiences of our predecessors, we can gain a sense of continuity and perspective, recognizing that we are part of a larger whole that extends beyond

---

[45] See James E. Bradley, Richard A. Muller, *Church History: An Introduction to Research Methods and Resources*, 2nd ed. (Grand Rapids, Cambridge: William B. Eerdmans Publishing Company, 2016), 56.

[46] See Jain, *Historical Method*, 7.

our individual experiences. Overall, history is a vital discipline that provides us with invaluable insights into the world around us and our place in it. It allows us to learn from the past, make sense of the present, and prepare for the future.

1.4.1.3. It Allows People to Analyze Their Own Age's Priorities and Accomplishments

The study of history offers people the opportunity to analyze and evaluate the priorities and achievements of their own era by providing them with a point of reference. By understanding the events and decisions that have shaped our world, individuals can gain perspective and insight into the challenges facing modern societies, rules, and businesses.[47] Through historical analysis, students can develop a deep understanding of how past events have influenced the present and gain a more complete understanding of the complexities of contemporary issues. This knowledge can empower individuals to make informed decisions and contribute to positive change in their communities and beyond.

1.4.2. Abuses

1.4.2.1. Labelling of "The Other"

Serageldin has raised concerns about the labelling of radical terrorists who claim to act in the name of Islam as "Muslim extremists" in the Western mass media. He believes that this labelling can be problematic.[48] This labelling, along with the media's obsessive focus on it, creates a false narrative that Muslims and Westerners share no common ground. This categorizing or labelling causes the existence of "the Other" which is a hindrance to world peace. This behaviour reinforces the idea of a "Clash of Civilizations" and can even lead to a self-fulfilling prophecy.[49]

[47] See Jain, *Historical Method*, 7.

[48] See Ismail Serageldin, "The Uses and Abuses of History," https://www.researchgate.net/publication/315700325_Uses_and_Abuses_of_history (17 Apr. 2024). Hereafter cited as Serageldin, "The Uses and Abuses."

[49] Serageldin, "The Uses and Abuses."

It is important to recognise that each person has a multifaceted identity that is both inherited and constructed.

Inherited characteristics such as race, gender, and mother tongue are largely outside of our control, while constructed characteristics like political affiliation, occupation, and geographic location are more fluid and tend to change over time. Religion is often acquired at a young age and is a significant part of many people's constructed identities. If an individual is unwilling to convert, their religion becomes a link between their inherited and constructed characteristics. Attempting to reduce an individual's complex identity to a single aspect, such as their religion, is not only inaccurate but also harmful.

Amin Maalouf has referred to these constructed identities as "murderous identities,"[50] especially when it comes to religion, where many individuals have strong emotional attachments. This fact has led Sen to argue that the religious partitioning of the world creates a profoundly misleading understanding of people worldwide and their diverse relationships.[51] It also has the effect of magnifying one distinction between people to the exclusion of all other significant concerns. It is essential to recognize the complexity of people's identities and the diversity that exists within and between different cultures and religions to build bridges between communities and foster greater understanding and cooperation.

1.4.2.2. The Making of Winners and Losers

According to Johnson Puthenpurackal, the desire of human beings to succeed and triumph over others is so strong that it often leads to the creation of 'truths' that are propagated for generations to come.[52] These so-called 'facts' are generated by narrators who have the power to shape their narratives in any manner they wish. The

[50] See Serageldin, "The Uses and Abuses," 7.

[51] Serageldin, "The Uses and Abuses," 7.

[52] See Johnson Puthenpurackal, "History as the Story of Victors: A Postmodern Reading," in *History and Historizing: Philosophical Reflections*, ed. by John Peter Vallabadoss (Bangalore: Asian Trading Corporation, 2012), 11, 12. Hereafter cited as Puthenpurackal, "History."

reliability of these producers determines the validity of the fact. Unfortunately, what benefits these producers is often promoted and pushed on to other people as if it were accurate and truthful. As a result of such dominating interaction, just a single point of view is considered the 'sole opinion,' while other points of view are drowned out by the louder viewpoint of the powerful ones.[53] This one-sided approach to facts and narratives has led to the suppression of alternative perspectives and has created a distorted version of reality that is often accepted as the truth.

1.4.2.3. History Writing as a Method to Sustain Oneself

Throughout the annals of history, there has been an unrelenting thirst for power and dominance amongst humanity. The pursuit of authority and superiority has been a driving force behind many of our actions, from the earliest civilizations to the present day. Our innate desire to establish ourselves as leaders, rulers, and managers of others has often led to the displacement or defeat of those who stand in our way. Even historians, who are tasked with the objective portrayal of events, have been known to skilfully craft narratives that elevate certain individuals or groups while diminishing the status of others.[54] This perpetual quest for prominence has shaped the course of civilization and continues to impact the world today.

1.4.2.4. Distortion for Political Purposes

The manipulation or fabrication of history is often used to serve political goals. Governments, leaders, and interest groups may deliberately interpret or rewrite history to support policies, legitimize power, or sway public opinion. This can result in the spread of false narratives that distort reality, such as legends, presumptions, and nationalist stories.

The Indian government, led by the Bharatiya Janata Party (B.J.P.), has granted the R.S.S. academic branch, the Vidhya Bharati Trust, permission to operate independently of the State Government's Educational Board and make curriculum

---

[53] Puthenpurackal, "History," 11, 12.

[54] See Puthenpurackal, "History," 13, 14.

modifications in schools. This has led to changes in the curriculum in Rajasthan, Madhya Pradesh, and Uttar Pradesh to give the R.S.S. more influence. The history textbooks have been altered to project the Hindutva perspective, with an emphasis on communal education and an attempt to Hinduize Indian history and culture. Additionally, the so-called Vedic Maths has been introduced[55] as a subject in academic settings.

In addition to academic instruction, Vidhya Bharati promotes a core curriculum that includes six subjects: Sanskrit, physical education, yoga, music, moral and spiritual education, and cultural understanding. Furthermore, the curriculum suggests that India's split was a result of a political conspiracy led by Christians.[56] These actions have come under scrutiny and criticism from various quarters, especially by those who argue that such modifications to the curriculum are an attempt to rewrite history in a way that supports a particular political ideology, rather than presenting facts objectively.

---

[55] See A. Pushparajan, "A Secular Critique of Hindutva," in *Hindutva: An Indian Christian Response,* ed. by J. Mattam, S.J., P. Arockiadoss, S.J. (Bangalore: Dharmaram Publications, 2002), 241. Hereafter cited as Pushparajan, "A Secular Critique."

[56] Pushparajan, "A Secular Critique," 242."

Chapter 2

Different Schools of History

The schools of history or the schools of historical interpretation focus on the analysis, scrutiny, reconstruction, and justification of historical events that have had an impact on people at a particular period. These institutions use various methods and perspectives to teach history. They employ several techniques for the interpretation and comprehension of global history. They all share the same objective of enhancing judgement and the course of humanity. The four main schools of history are Positivism, Historicism, Marxist History or Historical Materialism, and the Annales School.

2.1. Positivist School

A philosophical movement that emerged in Europe in the 19th and 20th centuries is known as positivism. The positivist school's specialists contend that knowledge is reliable when it results from observation and experience. They, therefore, sharply condemn superstition and speculation in the historical setting. The positivist movement and scientific sociology are credited to Auguste Comte (1798–1857),[57] who is also regarded as its originator. Comte sought

[57] See "4 Schools of Historical Interpretation And Their Characteristics - History – 2023," en.sperohope.com/4-escuelas-de-interpretaci-n-hist-rica-y-sus-caracter stic (17 Sep. 2023). Hereafter cited as "4 Schools of Historical."

to apply the same scientific observation of prevailing rules found in the natural sciences, or as he referred to them, "positive" sciences,[58] to the study of society. Leopold von Ranke's name also comes to the fore when one talks about Positivism.

For positivists, historical evidence does not need to be interpreted. It is founded on the idea that historical sources should be given the freedom to "speak for themselves" to help historians discover the unvarnished truth about the past. Historical positivists reject any further interpretation or analysis of the sources and concentrate on compiling them in their current state. They posit that history exists even without a historian.[59] They give more importance to facts than interpretation.

During the post-revolutionary era of France, when both France and Europe wished for a stable political system, Comte started to formulate the philosophy. There was also a strong incentive to create a social structure devoid of turmoil. To validate and advance hypotheses, positivism is founded on the scientific method. In this regard, scientists must refrain from adopting "common sense" and verify any material[60] before accepting it as reality.

The basis of positivism is the scientific method, which proposes and supports hypotheses. This school of thought uses science to understand social issues. Its core tenets are founded on the thorough research of the facts, precise and rigorous data, and the enrichment of history. It is a movement that looks for knowledge and social applications in a specific setting using exact sciences. According to Comte, the magical or religious and the metaphysical are two states that the human mind must pass through before it

---

[58] Arthur Marwick, *The Nature of History* (London: Macmilan Press, 1970), 41.

[59] See Lalfakawma Ralte, "Mizo Hnam Tobul, Kan Zik Chhuahna leh Kan Pem Kualna," in *Mizo Identity Bihchianna*, ed by B. Lalnunzira (Aizawl: SCMI, ATC Unit, 2019), 57.

[60] See Santiago Barlau, "Schools of Historical Interpretation and Their Characteristics," https://veintipico.com/schools-of-historical-interpretation-and ... (17 Sep. 2023). Hereafter cited as Santiago Barlau, "Schools of Historical Interpretation."

can form a reliable historical view.[61] Then, a positive state based on laws, observation, and experience is attained. The philosophy of Mr. Gradgrind precisely reflects this philosophy:[62]

> Now, what I want is, Facts…Facts alone are wanted in life. Plant nothing else, and root out everything else. You can only form the minds of reasoning animals upon Facts: nothing else will ever be of any service to them.

Historians set about gathering all the facts they could. As a result, there has been a massive rise in precise historical knowledge, based to an unprecedented degree on accurate and critical evaluation of evidence. This was the era that enriched history by compiling large amounts of meticulously filtered material.[63] The historians were content to continue discovering new facts because the area for discovery was limitless.

This new understanding of history was a lot more than the use of a new method; it was the dawning of a new mindset. Copernicus, Galileo, Newton, and the rest of the eighteenth-century scientific community gloriously declared that facts, not views, were authoritative. Partisanship, religious prejudice, hero worship, ambition, national passion, and pride of race or nation drove historians to distort or suppress the data at their disposal.[64] They did not share the scientists' veneration for facts.

Meanwhile, ordinary people became uninterested; they did not see why it mattered whether this or that information was uncovered or not, and a chasm steadily grew between the historian and ordinary intellectual people. Positivist philosophers protested that history was

---

[61] See "4 Schools of Historical," 2.

[62] "What does Mr. Gradgrind say is the most important philosophy?" https://www.enotes.com/homework-help/what-does-mr-gradgrind-say-is-the... (18 Sep. 2023).

[63] See R.G. Collingwood, *The Idea of History*, revised ed. (New Delhi: Oxford University Press, 2007), 127. Hereafter cited as Collingwood, *The Idea*.

[64] See James Westfall Thompson, *A History of Historical Writing Volume II: the Eighteenth and Nineteenth Centuries,* 3rd ed. (New York: Macmillan Company, 1954), 442.

not scientific if it stuck to facts; ordinary people objected that the facts it was bringing to light were dull[65] and unexciting.

In this context, Auguste Comte suggested that historical facts be exploited as the raw material for something more crucial and honestly fascinating than themselves. According to positivists, every natural science begins by establishing facts and then proceeds to find their causal relations. Accepting this assumption, Comte proposed a new science called sociology,[66] which would begin by discovering facts about human life and then go on to discover the causal connections between these facts.

Positivism's emphasis on objectivity and empirical evidence shaped the development of modern historical methodology, although its deterministic approach and neglect of social forces have been criticized by later scholars.

2.2. Historicist School or Historicism

The Historicist school of thought, which gained prominence in Germany during the 19th century, emphasized the contextual and interpretive nature of historical inquiry. Influenced by eminent scholars such as Johann Gustav Droysen, and Wilhelm Dilthey, adherents of this school rejected the positivist pursuit of objective truth. Instead, they focused on interpreting historical events within their cultural, social, and intellectual contexts. Historicists underscored the importance of interpretation and empathy in studying history, regarding it as a narrative shaped by human awareness and cultural forces. By challenging positivist assumptions and emphasizing the subjective nature of historical interpretation, Historicists established the framework for cultural and intellectual history.

From the emergence of romanticism in the late eighteenth century, historicism predominated in Germany. The fundamental tenet of historicism is that history shapes all cultures. This view that each group's traditions and beliefs are the results of that group's historical experience is symbolised by the term "historicism."

[65] See Collingwood, *The Idea,* 127.

[66] See Collingwood, *The Idea,* 128.

Nothing can be fully understood without reference to its history. Socrates' teachings, for example, could only be spread in the liberated environment of Athens. Customs and beliefs are like flowers that can only grow in a specific environment. The nation was stressed by historicists as the place where specific values were ingrained. As a result, Luther was revered in the church more as a German national hero than as a champion of the global reformation.[67] He personified the German nation's commitment, tenacity, and capacity for thinking.

How we value other groups except our own is a second theme in historicist theory. We are familiar with the traditions and values of the groups we are a part of. But how can we understand the importance of traditions and beliefs practised elsewhere? According to the historicist theory, people in other societies have values that are distinct from our own. People back then held distinct ideals as well. For a historian, the resulting issues are particularly serious. How can he or she penetrate the thought worlds of other places and times if he or she cannot leave his or her own? The historicist response is that we possess an intuitive or comprehending faculty.[68] Human beings possess the gift of empathy, which enables them to understand the importance of what other people do.

Vico explains the organic formation of societies, emphasises the division between sciences and humanities, and argues that there is a path to knowing primal and alien worlds of thinking by an ultimate and torturous effort of ingenious reconstruction.[69] He claims that by excruciating imagination and strenuous toil, we can reach out across history and enter the thoughts and sentiments of those long dead. We can recreate the lives and thoughts of other men and women whose culture is different from ours through creative empathy. Herder and Dilthey taught similar notions, speaking of the

---

[67] See David Bebbington, *Patterns in History* (Leicester: InterVarsity Press, 1979), 92, 93. Hereafter cited as Bebbington, *Patterns.*

[68] See Bebbington, *Patterns*, 92, 93.

[69] See Paul Avis, *Foundations of Modern Historical Thought: From Machiavelli to Vico* (London: Croom Helm Ltd., 1986), 133. Hereafter cited as Avis, *Foundations.*

historian recreating in his/her mind the spiritual experiences of the past[70] that are recorded in papers and other historical facts.

In contrast to positivism, historicism emphasises the significance of the historical interpretation that historians make of society and human destiny. Historicism rejects the notion that there are unchanging historical laws, in contrast to other schools of thought.[71] Historicism is the discipline that studies things, events, and phenomena from their inception to their conclusion. As opposed to exact sciences or universal rules, historicists rely more on the science of the spirit. According to this school, each historical fact is singular and unrepeatable, and history is viewed as a sort of global evolution.[72] It gives people a foundation upon which to study, examine, and comprehend history as a process with its own beginning, growth, and conclusion.

Vico asserted that historical understanding is a type of perception, a main manner of knowing the truth about reality that is considerably superior to mathematics and the exact sciences.[73] He began a new chapter of historical inquiry, that of philosophical romanticism or historicism. It is the notion of a science of mind whose method is the study of its evolution throughout history. Vico assumes that concepts evolve and that knowledge is a social process that can be tracked through the growth of a given culture's symbols and expressions, rather than a static network of everlasting, universal, obvious facts. It is learnt throughout by an understanding that the intuitive, the poetic, the mythopoetic, all of which some see as irrational, were the origins of creativity[74] in language, religion, and the formation of a community.

Vico's emphasis on rigorous empirical study is consistent with the overall attitude of the historical movement. Once he commented, "The useful historians are not those who give general descriptions of facts and explain them by reference to general

---

[70] See Avis, *Foundations*, 159, 160.

[71] See Santiago Barlau, "Schools of Historical Interpretation."

[72] See "4 Schools of Historical," 4.

[73] See Avis, *Foundations*, 136.

[74] See Avis, *Foundations*, 135.

conditions, but those who go into the greatest detail and reveal the particular cause of each event."[75]

Another prominent exponent of historicism is the German philosopher Johann Gottfried Herdel. Herdel contends that understanding a society's or an individual's behaviour stems from familiarity with its past. The invention of facts or events that did not actually occur to explain a phenomenon is one of the complaints levelled at this school; as a result, you cannot be certain of its veracity. Because it leaves room for conjecture, this detail lessens the persuasiveness of their arguments.[76] The historicist view that a person's capacity for reason defines them is flawed. History tends to undervalue how consistent human nature is.[77]

It is also debatable how we learn about the past according to the historicist theory. It is stated that the historian has insight into the minds of long-dead individuals. Therein lays its flaw. The degree to which the historian accurately portrays the past cannot be gauged by any objective standard. This issue does not exist, per romantic era historicists. Because intuition is personal, it has intrinsic advantages over imposing logical categories on the world of human beings. It seems that hazardous ideologies can flourish in historicism. The historians' conception of a beautiful German past provided a valuable resource for the Nazis. The issue here goes beyond the fact that historicism focused on the nation or that it had a right-wing predisposition to embrace what was conventional. More was alleged by the historicists. They frequently asserted that they had a responsibility to champion Germany's brilliance with one focus.[78] The nationalist excess of historians and statesmen was sparked by a questionable assertion about the importance of nationhood in the historical process.

---

[75] As cited in Avis, *Foundations*, 151.

[76] See "4 Schools of Historical," 7.

[77] See David Bebbington, *Patterns in History* (Leicester: InterVarsity Press, 1979), p. 114. Hereafter cited as Bebbington, *Patterns*.

[78] See Bebbington, *Patterns*, 114, 115.

2.3. Marxist History (Historical Materialism)

Frederick Engels coined the phrase "historical materialism," in 1892, which has been heavily influenced by Marxist and Leninist ideas.[79] Engels coined "historical materialism" as an equivalent for what he had also called "the materialist conception of history."[80] The goal of this type of interpretation is to comprehend global human history from an economic perspective. Marxism holds that the secret to historical change is how human beings construct their means of subsistence.[81] Marx's starting premise is that everyone is the author of his/her own history. People change their circumstances, and the educator must also be educated, according to the materialist view, which holds that people are products of their circumstances and upbringing and that transformed people are, therefore, products of new circumstances and new upbringing. Because of this, this ideology invariably leads to the division of society into two subgroups, each of which is superior to the other. Marx argues that the reality is that people are an integral component of the material world and play a role in its creation.[82] Historical materialism's foundation was established in this way.

Based on the ideas of German economist Karl Marx, Engels incorporated economic elements like labour relations, production methods, and labour practises into his historical interpretation. These elements significantly influenced how the world's historical events were perceived. The tenets of historical materialism are based on the assertion that economics has played a crucial role in shaping humanity's history. Most of the time, history must be described in terms of a class struggle, according to supporters of this Marxist ideology. Now, this university is regarded as a starting point for explaining historical economic occurrences. Since not every historical event lends itself to materialist interpretation, it

---

[79] See Santiago Barlau, "Schools of Historical Interpretation," 4.

[80] Z. A. Jordan, *The Evolution of Dialectical Materialism: A Philosophical and Sociological Analysis* (London: Macmillan, 1967), 37.

[81] See Bebbington, *Patterns*, 117.

[82] See Bebbington, *Patterns*, 121, 122.

must occasionally be used.[83] It is advisable to consult various schools to obtain more unbiased judgements, even when historical study supports a materialistic approach.

2.4. The Annales School

In 1929, Lucien Febvre and Marc Bloch established the School of the Annales in France. It has a reputation for being one of the most significant historical currents of the twentieth century, particularly in French history. The current's first tenets and ideas were published in a reputable publication at the time, and soon after that, it became a historiographic current. The name of the publication was *Annales de la Historia*.[84] Their interest in the experience of time that was unmistakably relevant to the twentieth century was mixed with their goals to construct an integrated, whole history that was attentive to the diversity of geography and the complexities of human outlook[85] or mind.

This school is more interested in history from a social perspective than from the perspective of political and personal events in human history. The social sciences' methodology serves as the foundation for the Annales stream. This school's historians write history to address questions and offer solutions to issues. It is, therefore, somewhat compared to the precise natural sciences. In contrast to classical historiography, historians of this school interpret history thoroughly rather than writing about the past. They begin with their own arbitrary conceptions to analyse historical facts. The School of the Annales is fascinated with the finer points of societies as well as the in-depth analysis of historical events. It considers a variety of factors, including attire, regional languages, musical instruments, and social customs.[86] Additionally, it contains information about the field of mentality research, which

[83] See Santiago Barlau, "Schools of Historical Interpretation," 5.

[84] See "4 Schools of Historical," 7.

[85] See Michael Roberts, "The Annales School and Historical Writing," in *Making History: An Introduction to the History and Practices of a Discipline,* edited by Peter Lambert and Phillipp Schofield (Abingdon: Routledge, 2004), 78.

[86] See "4 Schools of Historical," 8.

examines how human beings in the past might have reasoned, thought, and behaved.[87] This field draws on approaches from philosophy, psychology, art, anthropology, and history.

In conclusion, the study of history can be divided into four distinct intellectual traditions, namely the Positivist, Historicist, Marxist, and Annales schools. Each of these schools has contributed valuable insights into historical interpretation and methodology. However, it is also important to note that each school has its own limitations and biases that reflect their respective contexts and theoretical frameworks. As such, it is of utmost importance for scholars to critically engage with these historiographical traditions to gain a more nuanced understanding of the past and contribute to the ongoing debates within the discipline of history. By doing so, they can expand their knowledge, refine their research, and make meaningful contributions to the field of history.

---

[87] See Santiago Barlau, "Schools of Historical Interpretation," 5.

Chapter 3

Historical Sources and Their Significances

Traditionally, sources of information are frequently categorized as primary, secondary, and tertiary data. However, with the coming of sources like electronic and Artificial Intelligence (A.I.), we have now postmodern or ultra-postmodern sources at hand. Apart from these, oral tradition also comes into play when one talks about sources of historical accounts. The originality of the content and the proximity to the source or origin are the bases for these classifications. This lets the reader know whether the author is giving first-person accounts of events or is giving the experiences and viewpoints of others, which is referred to as second-hand knowledge.

3.1. Primary Sources

Primary data are materials collected from individuals being examined or from people involved in an incident being examined. This is what Mabry called "the "pure gold" of research data.[88] Primary sources are unique artefacts or records that were produced during the period being considered. Examples include historical and legal papers, letters, diaries, family records, speeches, interviews, autobiographies, films, government documents,

---

[88] See Hunter P. Mabry, *A Manual for Researchers and Writers*, 2nd ed. (Bangalore: BTESSC, 2011), 92. Hereafter cited as Mabry, *A Manual*.

eyewitness accounts, experiment results, statistical data,[89] creative writing pieces, and artefacts. Primary sources are writings that were produced contemporaneously with the period or topic being examined, or very nearly contemporaneously. They are the fundamental components that give historians information[90] and raw data they need.

3.1.1. Sub-dividing Primary Sources

Primary sources can be sub-divided into different categories, such as:

3.1.1.1. Documents of an Immediate Nature

Records of people who are involved in daily life are kept in the form of memoranda, bills, deeds, charters, records of parliaments and congresses, newspaper reports, pamphlets and broadsides, popular poetry, graffiti, and other materials. Chronicles, histories, biographies, autobiographies, and contemporary character profiles[91] and manuscripts[92] are some examples of documents of an immediate nature.

3.1.1.2. Theoretical Treatises (Archives/Records)

The writings of theoretical treatises always display thoughtful and sober planning, design, and argumentation. Whatever the topic, it is expected that the writer will be more concerned with values that are deeper, farther-reaching, and more eternal than is the case with evidence of an immediate kind. While immediate credentials, documents, and papers may undoubtedly show careful forethought and deeply held views, the explicit goal of a theoretical treatise is to construct and define a core value that the author believes to be true.[93]

---

[89] See "What is a Primary Source," https://guides.library.harvard.edu/HistSciInfo/primary (19 Sep. 2023), 1. Hereafter cited as "What is a Primary Source."

[90] See Norman F. Cantor, Richard I Schneider, *How to Study History* (Illinois: AHM Publishing Corporation, 1967), 22, 23. Hereafter cited as Cantor, *How to Study History*.

[91] See Cantor, *How to Study History*, 39, 40.

[92] See "What is a Primary Source," 2.

[93] See Cantor, *How to Study History,* 40.

Letters, sketches made by eyewitnesses, notes, private journals, diaries, and other similar items can all be discovered in archival collections.

The two categories mentioned above both include first-person narratives written by people who lived through the events and concepts the source describes. These stories could have been casual, spontaneous, and only meant for private use, or they could have been deliberately prepared, formal in nature,[94] and frequently intended for a public audience.

Statistical information is a unique type of evidence since it is derived from writings and recordings from earlier times rather than being a direct representation of them. Consequently, when working with statistics, one should exercise extreme caution because, despite having a very realistic appearance, their methods of collection may alter the meaning they represent.[95] It is important to resist the urge to believe numbers to be unquestionably true and factual.

3.1.1.3. Literature and Non-verbal Materials

Literary materials are invaluable for offering insight into tastes, temperaments, styles, and ideas of an age. Literary materials include books, periodicals, poems, memoirs, autobiographies,[96] novels, plays, diaries, etc.

Nonverbal materials include some that scholars have traditionally recognised as legitimate sources, e.g., the evidence offered by coins and by archaeology, but historians should give more attention to some kinds of nonverbal artefacts[97] like paintings, sculpture, and music.

3.1.2. Where to Find Primary Sources

The non-literary sources, such as tombs, historic structures and monuments, entire towns and cities, artefacts, coins, inscriptions,

[94] See Cantor, *How to Study History*, 40.

[95] See Cantor, *How to Study History*, 41.

[96] See "What is Literary Source?" https://edurev.in/question/3095891/ (19 Sep. 2023).

[97] See Cantor, *How to Study History*, 41.

etc., are the most easily accessible primary sources. People are a second category of primary sources. Interviewing people about events in which they took part or watched is a useful method to use them as primary sources. Published collections of chosen materials are the most prevalent written sources. Larger and more well-known collections, such as those found in state archives, well-funded universities, or public libraries,[98] are available in addition to these sources.

3.1.3. Considerations in Dealing with Primary Sources

When using primary sources, there are some things to keep in mind. A historian needs to be confident that they are properly equipped to comprehend a primary source. That implies that he or she can understand what the source's words imply and the context of any allusions that are made, either expressly or implicitly. Even if a historian believes he/she is a natural speaker of the language, any document from a time earlier than their own communicates to them in a language that is substantially different from their own.[99] Changes and evolution of language come into play here.

It is best to read primary sources in the context of values that were prevalent at the time the source was written. It is crucial to study the viewpoints expressed in primary sources. Historians must go beyond just comparing these values to their contemporary ones to comprehend the significance of some major opinions.[100] To properly understand the function of the main source in its era, they should attempt to tie primary opinions to the entirety of their contemporary context.

The editors pick the materials that, in their opinion, are significant or illustrative of the period or subject that interests them. Regarding whether they have selected the greatest documents, there will undoubtedly be a valid dispute. Therefore, edited primary

[98] See John C. B. Webster, *An Introduction to History,* 2nd ed. (Delhi: Macmillan, 1981), 66, 67. Hereafter cited as Webster, *An Introduction.*

[99] See Cantor, *How to Study History,* 41, 42.

[100] See Cantor, *How to Study History,* 42, 43.

source collections can only provide a partial picture of the period[101] or subject being discussed.

Consideration must be given to a source's veracity by historians. They must determine whether the document they are holding is an earlier version, a copy, or the original. If it is a copy or a later version, it should be compared to the original to determine whether it is authentic and unaltered or whether it has been edited or changed.

Some materials do not neatly fall into the primary or secondary source category; some are primary sources from one perspective while being secondary from another. The autobiography stands out as a prime example. An autobiography frequently assumes the proportions of both a main account of the writer's own experiences and views and a secondary history of the eras through which he has lived.[102] It is frequently cited in bibliographies as a primary source.

An autobiography is typically written several weeks, months or years after the events it describes, therefore it should typically be viewed with even more caution than the simpler source text. According to K. L. Khurana, many memoirs and autobiographies are written by people nearing the end of their lives.[103] At this point, the author's memory is not as sharp as it once was, thus he/she records all his/her life events based on declining recollection, so they cannot be entirely trusted.

3.2. Secondary Sources

Secondary sources can be identified in terms of their time relationship to the subject being studied; a secondary work for a subject discusses the subject but is written after the time contemporary with it. All secondary sources will be based on primary sources, and most will include reports of information

---

[101] See Webster, *An Introduction*, 68.

[102] See Arthur Marwick, *The Nature of History* (London: Macmillan, 1970), 134.

[103] K. L Khurana, *Concepts and Methods of Historiography*, 8th ed. (Agra: Lakhsmi Narain Agarwal, 2017), 101.

derived from primary sources.[104] Secondary sources are the works that contain the explications of, and judgments on this primary material.

In other words, a secondary source is a critical analysis and explanation of a primary source. It might present a study of historical occurrences and primary sources that have not been studied before or a fresh take on previously examined ones. Another option for a secondary source is to combine the work of other historians to create a whole new interpretation.

Secondary data are materials concerning other people or events in which the authors did not take part. Secondary data would often include interpretations of other people's thoughts, census data, opinion polls, and oral traditions. A researcher investigating a specific indigenous community would generally consider information written by a member of that group regarding the life and culture of that group to be primary data, while material written by someone outside the group would normally be considered secondary data.[105] A person from outside the community would hardly provide or write primary evidence.

3.2.1. Where to Find Secondary Sources?

Secondary sources may be obtained from libraries, bookstores, news sites, and online databases. Longer analyses of the subject may also be found in book chapters, journal articles, or even as separate monographs.[106] In a specialised encyclopaedia, we can learn about the subject and review the bibliography at the end of the entry.

3.2.2. Significance of Secondary Sources

The arrangement of events and the justification of their significance by defining linkages of cause and effect among them should result from the examination and elucidation of primary sources. This is the

---

[104] See Cantor, *How to Study History,* 23.

[105] See Hunter P. Mabry, *A Manual for Researchers and Writers,* 2nd ed. (Bangalore: BTESSC, 2011), 93. Hereafter cited as Mabry, *A Manual.*

[106] See "Types of Sources and Where to Find Them: Secondary Sources," https://www.library.illinois.edu/hpnl/tutorials/secondary-sources (21 Sept. 2023).

crucial point at which history is constructed. History's purpose is to show the significance of the facts by illuminating their origins and causes. In other words, a historian's goal is to produce a secondary source of their own, one that has a historiographical topic or point of view[107] rather than just reporting what is in primary sources.

Secondary literature is frequently an excellent source of primary information. Primary sources can occasionally be hard to locate or may not even be published. In similar situations, one might have to rely on summaries of primary materials and quotations that have been excerpted. There are footnotes and quotations from unpublished treatises in certain secondary source volumes. There are gold mines[108] of primary sources in those works. In addition to the references to and quotations from primary sources, one may come across statistical information that is quite helpful, such as inventories of supplies, records, or harvests, a description of how long a particular military operation took, and so on.

3.2.3. Things to Consider while Using Secondary Sources

You must be aware that your source material is someone else's opinion and not the plain truth when you use other historians' inferences as if they were facts. Many of us frequently allude to important historical notions as if they were shown to be true. One is not referencing or quoting a fact when they are citing or quoting words. One must keep in mind that one is merely quoting an interpretation or an inferential hypothesis and that other historians' writings may present different interpretations of how the facts relate to one another. It is important to use critical judgment while evaluating the interpretation being used.[109] Such a strategy will demonstrate that the person is aware of the distinction between a fundamental fact and a hypothetical verdict.

The facts of history are always filtered via the imagination of the recorder and never presented to us in their purest form since they do not and cannot exist in that state. As a result, when reading a

---

[107] See Cantor, *How to Study History,* 91, 92.

[108] See Cantor, *How to Study History,* 91, 92.

[109] See Cantor, *How to Study History,* 94.

historical work, we should be more concerned with the historian who produced it than with the historical data it includes.[110] The strongest defence against blindly accepting one historical perspective is to read as many of its key works on a given historical period or issue as you can. Reading a variety of secondary sources on the same issue will make it clear that there are often multiple ways to understand how some fundamental facts relate to one another.[111] Anyone considering conducting any type of advanced research in the history subject ought to make it a habit to read extensively and consistently every day.

When reading any secondary work, the reader's initial goal should be to identify the book's major argument or the premises and standards on which the authors have built their findings. That is why Carr encouraged us to "study the historian before you begin to study the facts."[112] Furthermore, reading the book in the original language is necessary for gaining complete comprehension of a secondary source.[113] Even the greatest translations frequently alter the connotations.

3.3. Tertiary Sources

These are sources that index, abstract, organize, compile, or digest other sources. Some reference materials and textbooks are considered tertiary sources when their chief purpose is to list, summarize or simply repackage ideas or other pieces of information. Tertiary sources are usually not credited to a particular author.[114] An index or textual compilation of primary and secondary sources is referred to as a tertiary source.

---

[110] See E. H. Carr, *What is History?* (England: Penguin Books, 1961), 22. Hereafter cited as

[111] See Cantor, *How to Study History,* 95.

[112] Carr, *What is History?* 23.

[113] See Cantor, *How to Study History,* 101, 102.

[114] See Mark Brilliant, "Primary, Secondary, and Tertiary Sources in History," https://history.berkeley.edu/sites/default/files/history_source_ty... (20 Sept. 2023). Hereafter cited as Brilliant, "Primary."

3.3.1. Examples of Tertiary Sources

Dictionaries, encyclopaedias (may also be secondary), almanacks, fact books, Wikipedia, bibliographies (may also be secondary), directories, guidebooks, manuals, handbooks, and textbooks (maybe secondary), indexing and abstracting sources,[115] concordances, manuals, textbooks, directories, indexes, and timelines are some examples of tertiary sources.

It also includes books and essays that are solely based on secondary sources or the work of others. Tertiary sources are typically synthetic and copied in nature, that is, they combine various independent but connected stories of a specific event, problem, and body of scholarship. By using tertiary sources, we can get a lot of information, making them useful places to start our study. Tertiary materials frequently have footnotes pointing researchers to the right path[116] concerning secondary sources.

3.3.2. Considerations while Dealing with Tertiary Sources

A bibliography, dictionary, or encyclopaedia may be used as a secondary or tertiary source, depending on the subject or research, by a scholar. Because of this, it is challenging to categorise many sources as either one category or the other. The line separating a secondary source from a tertiary source might vary among academic disciplines.

Although secondary sources are frequently reliable, they lack the specialised information that scholarly sources are supposed to supply and are frequently not assigned to a single author. Because of these factors, you probably would not credit tertiary sources in your research report,[117] though you may still use them in the background.

To build background information, find pertinent phrases and terms, comprehend current disputes in your subject, and identify

---

[115] See "What are the Differences?" https://crk.umn.edu/library/primary-secondary-and-tertiary-sources, (20 Sept. 2023).

[116] See Brilliant, "Primary," 1.

[117] See Eoghan Ryan, "Tertiary Sources Explained | Quick Guide & Examples," www.scribbr.com/working-with-sources/tertiary-sources/ (20 Sept. 2023). Hereafter cited as Ryan, "Tertiary Sources."

significant scholars, use tertiary sources early on in your research process. This will serve as the basis for future research and point you in the direction of valuable primary and secondary sources[118] that you will use in-depth during the writing process.

3.4. Postmodern Sources

Postmodern sources of information are those that challenge the assumptions and values of modernism, such as rationality, objectivity, and universal truth. Postmodern sources of information may include literary texts, internet media, philosophical discourses, and cultural practices that emphasize relativism, scepticism, and ideology.

3.4.1. Some Examples of Postmodern Sources of Information

Social networking uses internet-based social media platforms to connect with friends, family, or peers. Some of the most popular social networking sites include Facebook, Instagram, TikTok, WhatsApp, and X. Marketers use social networking to increase brand recognition and encourage brand loyalty. Internet, television, radio, ChatGPT, blogs, Geo-fencing.

The internet is an invaluable source of information, offering a wealth of data on virtually any topic imaginable. From online newspapers and magazines to blogs, forums, and social media websites, the internet offers a wealth of sources for research[119] and staying up-to-date on current events.

3.4.2. Considerations While Using Postmodern Sources

The impact of postmodernism on various fields, such as literature, philosophy, sociology, and cultural studies, has been significant. The fundamental tenets of postmodernism are centred around the rejection of grand narratives and the recognition of the subjective nature of knowledge formation. Given the increasing reliance on postmodern sources by academics, it is imperative to critically evaluate their use in scholarly discourse.

---

[118] See Ryan, "Tertiary Sources," 1.

[119] See "What are the 10 Different Sources of Information?" https://edupepper.com/what-are-the-10-different-sources-of-information/ (20 Sept. 2023).

We will try to analyze the critical issues that arise when engaging with postmodern texts to assist researchers in navigating the complexities of postmodernism. The evaluation of postmodern sources must be approached with caution, and scholars must be cognizant of the unique challenges posed by the postmodern paradigm.

In particular, the rejection of grand narratives is often accompanied by a proliferation of micro-narratives, which can be challenging to navigate. Additionally, the subjective nature of knowledge formation can lead to a relativistic approach that is at odds with traditional scholarly practices. Scholars must be aware of these issues and develop appropriate strategies for evaluating postmodern sources.

Overall, the analysis of postmodern texts is a crucial skill for scholars in various fields. By understanding the critical issues involved in engaging with postmodernism, researchers can navigate the complexities of this paradigm and incorporate postmodern sources in a meaningful and appropriate manner.

3.4.2.1. Authorial Voice and Subjectivity

Postmodern sources emphasise the subjective experiences and opinions of writers. In contrast to traditional texts, which prioritise objectivity and authorial authority, postmodern works blur the line between fact and fiction. This requires researchers to critically evaluate the credibility of sources. It is crucial to recognise the inherent subjectivity in postmodern tales and approach them with a sophisticated awareness of the author's perspective and objectives.

3.4.2.2. Rejection of the Idea of a Single, Objective Reality in Favour of Multiple Perspectives

As a result, when using postmodern sources, researchers must recognize the variety of perspectives expressed in these writings. This requires a thorough examination that considers opposing interpretations and alternative narratives, thereby expanding the research discourse with a variety of views.

3.4.2.3. Fluidity of Meaning

Postmodern literature values ambiguity and open-endedness over definite meanings. This means that the meaning acquired from postmodern sources is naturally flexible and context-dependent. Researchers must be aware of the dynamic nature of meaning in postmodern literature, recognising that interpretations can shift over time and in different socio-cultural situations. This necessitates a reflexive approach to analysis in which scholars critically engage with the intricacies of meaning-making processes.

3.4.2.4. Validation and Academic Rigour

Postmodernism lacks a fixed truth paradigm, making it challenging for scholars to evaluate sources and preserve academic rigour. Unlike traditional procedures, which prioritise empirical data and logical consistency, postmodern approaches place a premium on deconstructing and destabilising hegemonic narratives. Researchers must use novel ways to examine the credibility of postmodern sources, such as investigating intertextuality, contextualizing within theoretical frameworks, and critically evaluating the rhetorical strategies used by authors.

Working with postmodern texts requires a comprehensive knowledge of the difficulties that underpin postmodern ideology. By critically evaluating concerns such as authorial voice, variety of views, fluidity of meaning, and validation techniques, researchers can effectively incorporate postmodern sources into scholarly discourse while maintaining academic rigour. Furthermore, accepting the challenges offered by postmodernism allows scholars to enrich their studies and contribute to ongoing discussions in their particular domains.

3.5. Oral Sources

Oral history is a field of study that aims to collect, preserve, and interpret the experiences and statements of individuals, communities, and participants in past events. It is one of the oldest forms of historical inquiry, dating back to a time before writing was invented. At the same time, it is also one of the most modern, with recording devices being used since the 1940s and modern electronic devices[120] being employed in the present day.

Oral sources play a crucial role in understanding human experiences, cultural customs, and historical events. Unlike written records that may contain biases or omissions, oral sources offer direct access to personal narratives and community memory. They help diversify viewpoints, challenge prevailing narratives, and elevate marginalized voices, making them an essential part of academic research.

3.5.1. Significances

Oral sources allow researchers to gain insight into subjective viewpoints and lived experiences of individuals, communities, and social groups. They capture nuances and personal insights not effectively preserved in written records, helping to create a more in-depth understanding of varied perspectives and socio-cultural contexts by focusing on participant voices.

Oral traditions such as folklore, mythology, and oral literature are vital components of cultural heritage, retaining intangible cultural traditions, language intricacies, and collective memories that would otherwise be lost or marginalized. Researchers who document and analyze oral traditions help to preserve and revitalize cultural legacy, supporting intergenerational transmission and cultural continuity.

Oral sources provide different viewpoints and counter-narratives to standard historical accounts. They offer essential insights into marginalized experiences, resistance movements, and subaltern voices, especially in contexts where written records are few or biased. Including oral accounts can help scholars reveal overlooked events, elevate marginalized perspectives, and create more inclusive historical narratives.

---

[120] See "Oral History Defined," http://oralhistory.org/about/do-oral-history/ (as of April 6, 2024).

3.5.2. Considerations

Using oral sources requires methodological rigour and ethical awareness. Researchers must consider informed consent, confidentiality, and power relations when working with participants. Factors like interviewer bias, memory distortion, and oral tradition dynamics must be carefully considered to maintain the integrity and validity of oral data. By following ethical norms and using rigorous methodological frameworks, researchers can ensure the authenticity and integrity of their findings.

Oral histories can be valuable sources of information. However, it is important to keep in mind that memories can be flawed. When using these records as primary sources, it is crucial to consider that the person may have been influenced by other people's accounts, literature, or even videos about the events they are recalling.[121] In general, the more closely related the narrative is to the events described, the more reliable it is considered.

In summary, oral sources are excellent resources for academic research, providing insights into lived experiences, cultural practices, and historical contexts. However, using oral sources requires methodological rigour, ethical awareness, and critical reflexivity. By recognizing the importance of oral sources, scholars contribute to a more inclusive, multifaceted understanding of human history, culture, and society.

Historical research is a complex endeavour that requires the use of a diverse array of sources, each presenting unique perspectives and challenges. The ability to critically assess and triangulate multiple sources is essential for the creation of intricate, evidence-based interpretations of the past. The application of interdisciplinary approaches and the utilization of digital technologies can enrich historical study and broaden our understanding of human history. By embracing these practices, historians can enhance the quality and scope of their scholarship, contributing to the advancement of historical knowledge and the dissemination of accurate, evidence-based accounts of the past.

---

[121] See https://www.library.illinois.edu/village/primarysource/mod1/pg11.htm (6 Apr. 2024).

Chapter 4

World History and History of Christianity

Christianity has had an indelible impact on social, and economic status procedures, standards, and beliefs throughout the world. It has affected artwork, construction, literary works, learning, and community morals, hence shaping national and civilizational identities. The advancement of Christian theology, the formation of educational institutions by monastic orders, and the church's support of art have all contributed to the richness of human civilization. Furthermore, Christianity has played an important role in developing legal and moral structure, campaigning for fairness, equality, and humanitarian issues.

Christianity's history has been marked by both amicable and conflictual interactions with various civilizations and customs of faith. Christianity's spread is frequently associated with activities of colonialism, imperialism, and cultural assimilation, resulting in conflicts and disputes with indigenous cultures and belief systems. It did, however, allow cross-cultural contacts, dialogue, and idea exchange, all of which contributed to the enhancement of the global heritage of culture.

This chapter provides an illuminating comparison of secular and Christian history, highlighting both their parallels and differences. While secular history generally documents events using scientific data and academic investigation, Christian history weaves religious ideas and narratives into historical events, frequently evaluating them using a theological perspective.

4.1. Similarities

First, both secularism and Christianity share a common ground in their emphasis on individual freedom and the value of community. Christianity teaches that surrendering to God's plans and obeying God's commands is vital for our well-being, but it also recognizes that every individual has free will[122] and can make their own decisions. Similarly, secularism views individual freedom as a crucial aspect of human liberty.

Secondly, both perspectives highlight the significance of community. For Christians, this is often manifested through church attendance and building relationships with fellow Christians. On the other hand, secularists may engage in social activities or contribute to charitable organizations that promote societal causes.[123] The sense of belonging to a group reinforces their ties as members.

Thirdly, community plays a significant role in Christianity as it fosters spiritual growth and provides support for individuals. Through worship, fasting, sharing personal experiences, and forming meaningful relationships, Christians find comfort and guidance to navigate life's challenges. In secularism, where religious beliefs do not factor in, people come together based on shared interests or ideas.[124] This may include political views or neighbourhood groups, where the sense of belonging to a community reinforces their connection as members.

Fourthly, both communities embrace inclusiveness, and welcome everyone regardless of colour or origin, thereby creating an environment in which diversity is valued rather than despised. This has been observed all around the world, with churches

---

[122] See Adam Philips, "Similarities Between Secularism and Christianity," https://thewitness.org/similarities-between-secularism-and-Christianity/ (11 Apr. 2024). Hereafter cited as Philips, "Similarities."

[123] See Philips, "Similarities," 1.

[124] See Philips, "Similarities." 1.

welcoming refugees seeking sanctuary in foreign countries and varied organizations banding together beyond ethnic boundaries to protest injustices such as police violence against minorities.

Fifthly, one of the shared values between secularism and Christianity is their commitment to promoting justice and compassion for all. They both seek to create a society where people are treated with dignity, regardless of their beliefs or background, and where harmony prevails over violence.

Sixthly, throughout human history, both secular and Christian societies have been shaped by a diverse range of influential figures, such as kings, prophets, priests, and religious leaders. These individuals have played a significant role in shaping the cultural, political, and religious landscapes of their respective communities. Kings, through their power and authority, have influenced the direction of their kingdom's development. Prophets, revered for their divine insights and revelations, have provided guidance and direction to entire nations. Priests and religious leaders have also played an essential role in shaping society, serving as moral guides and spiritual leaders who help people navigate life's challenges and develop a deeper understanding of their faith. The impact of these influential figures has been profound, shaping the course of history in countless ways.

Seventhly, Christianity is a religious doctrine that emphasises the belief that the attainment of salvation is only possible through Jesus Christ. According to Christian teachings, Jesus is the son of God, and his crucifixion and subsequent resurrection provide humanity with a means of redemption from sin and mortality. In contrast, Islam is a monotheistic faith that also affirms the existence of one God, Allah, with Muslims regarding Muhammad as his final prophet. While there are some shared beliefs between Christianity and Islam, such as the belief in one God, we can also see some significant disparities in their beliefs and practices.

Finally, both the Christian and secular communities recognize the significance of environmental conservation. Christians consider it a moral responsibility to care for God's creations, while secularists refer to it as climate change and advocate for preserving the earth for future generations. These shared principles provide a common ground for collaboration towards positive changes in our communities and beyond. The goal is to create sustainable and long-lasting improvements that benefit everyone, whether it is through safeguarding human rights or preserving the environment. We must work together towards this cause, with a focus on implementing technical solutions to mitigate climate change and protect our planet from further damage.

4.2. Differences

Firstly, secular history is an investigation of societies, civilizations, happenings, and advancements without a religious bias. It may encompass research on diverse civilizations, empires, battles, trends in society, financial structures, technological developments, and so on. The history of Christianity explores its beginnings, development, doctrines, practices, and influence as a religious tradition. It delves into the ministry of Jesus Christ, the beginnings of the Christian Church, doctrinal debates, the expansion of Christianity, encounters with other faiths and civilizations, Christianity's role in moulding communities, and its influence on culture, literature, governance, and ideologies.

Secondly, secular history encompasses a broad range of geographical locations, historical periods, and topics, which include, but are not limited to, Christianity. The History of Christianity, however, is a specialized field that concentrates exclusively on the Christian faith, its followers, establishments, and interactions within the framework of global history. It examines the development of Christianity, its impact on society, and the role of the Church in shaping the course of human events. It is important to note that while secular history is a comprehensive study of human civilization, it does not focus exclusively on Christianity. Instead, it covers various aspects of human life, such as culture, politics, economics, art, and science. On the other hand, the History of Christianity is a specialized field that delves deep into the origins, evolution, and influence of the Christian religion. Therefore, it is essential to distinguish between the two fields, as each has its own scope, methodology, and objectives. While secular history provides a broader understanding of human civilization, the History of Christianity offers a more specialized and in-depth analysis of the Christian faith and its impact on the world.

Thirdly, secular historians use various sources, such as archaeological data, written documents, oral traditions, and artefacts, to piece together the past. Historians of Christianity also employ these sources, but they generally focus on religious literature, theological works, ecclesiastical records, and other Christian-specific materials. They may use religion-specific approaches like textual analysis, hermeneutics, and comparative religious studies.

Fourthly, secular history aims for neutrality and objectivity by analysing historical occurrences and changes using evidence rather than predetermined views or prejudices. Theological viewpoints, spiritual obligations, and theological prejudices can all influence interpretations of Christian history. Historians may perceive historical events and figures differently based on their religious allegiance.

Fifthly, secular history is frequently investigated and instructed in academic contexts, to present an in-depth comprehension of the evolution of humanity to a wide range of listeners. Researchers, biblical scholars, religious leaders, and others interested in the history of faith or the Christian religion may find the history of Christianity particularly interesting.[125] It contributes to an improved comprehension of Christian beliefs, methods, and their relation to the past.

Sixthly, secular history follows cyclical ideas. It depends on the maxim, "History repeats itself," that is, repetition after repetition. Origen criticized this by saying that he was not sure how secular historians could sustain their stance by claiming that worlds emerge from time to time that are not different from one another but are equal in every way. For if there is said to be a world similar in all respects (to the present), then Adam and Eve will do the same things that they did before: there will be a second deluge, and the same Moses will lead a nation of nearly 600,000 out of Egypt; Judas will also betray the Lord a second time; Paul will wear the clothes of those who stoned Stephen a second time, and everything that has

[125] See Philips, "Similarities," 1.

happened in this life will be said to be repeated - a situation that, in his opinion, cannot be established by any reasoning if souls are actuated by free will and preserve either their progression or reversal according to the power of their will. For souls are not forced on in a cycle that repeats after several generations to the same round, to do or seek this or that; rather, they steer the trajectory of their acts wherever the freedom of their own choice leads them.[126] This is inharmonious with history. The cyclical notion is more efficiently articulated in the Hindu notion of the *Mahagaya/Mahayuga,* or the Great Cycle, as chronicled in the Puranas.

The Hindu philosophy of the history of human beings revolves around the concept of a complete cycle, also known as *mahayuga*, that takes place within the context of the universe. This cycle is further divided into *yugas*, or ages, with the longest of them occurring at the start and the shortest at the end. As the generations pass, the morality, equity, pleasure, and affluence of human beings decline, ultimately leading to the annihilation of everything after the last *yuga*.[127] However, certain contemporary authors suggest that the situation may not be as disastrous as it seems. According to Mundadan, by adopting Eliades' perspective on the matter, one can understand that the Hindu conception of never-ending cycles of creation and annihilation can serve as an instrument for gaining understanding and a way to fulfil humanity's longing to transcend individual and historical time and enter the Mystical Great Time. Through myths, human beings can emerge from their ignorance and begin to associate reality with their appearance or possessions. They are elevated from the plane of mundane daily life to the Real, which leads to a deeper understanding of the nature of existence.[128] Therefore, the Hindu philosophy of the cyclical nature of human

---

[126] "What the Allegorist Origen Taught About Adam and Eve," htpps://www.johnsanidopoulos.com/2012/01/what-allegorist-origen-taught-about.html (11 Apr. 2024).

[127] See Mircea Eliade, *Images and Symbols: Studies in Religious Symbolism* (London: Harvill Press, 1961), 60-70.

[128] See A. M. Mundadan, CMI, *History and Beyond* (Kerala: Jeevass Publications, 1997), 53, 54.

history can be seen to help human beings connect with their true selves and the world around them.

Whereas the history of Christianity follows linear theory. It seeks the end of the world in which God will re-create the whole creation. The Christian community's salvation narrative centred upon the doctrine of creation, the fall of human beings, salvation, and the last coming, which signals the end of all of civilization.[129] This is the reason why Christian historians give prominence to future events.[130] It portrays history progressing from the distant past to the future.

Seventhly, Christianity's core tenet is that redemption is possible only through the grace of Christ. This necessitates that the life, teachings, and ministry of Jesus hold a preeminent position in Christian theology, as they form the nucleus of the faith's teachings based on the Bible.[131] Conversely, Hinduism, among other religions, has a vast pantheon of deities, with millions of gods and goddesses venerated across different regions and sects. This fundamental difference in the concept of divinity is one of the key distinctions between Christianity and many other world religions.

Eighthly, Christianity's fundamental tenet is that the world was created by God. This belief derives from the notion that God is the ultimate source of all existence and that God fashioned the universe from nothing. Conversely, many secular historians subscribe to the Big Bang theory, which posits that the universe arose from a singularity, a point of infinite density and temperature, approximately 13.8 billion years ago. This theory is bolstered by a wealth of empirical data, including cosmic microwave background radiation, the observed distribution of galaxies, and the abundance of light elements in the universe. Despite these divergent worldviews, both religious and secular

---

[129] Cf. Margareth Chatterjee, "The Meaning of History: Principal Miller Endowment Lecture," in *Journal of the Madras University*, XLVII/2 (July, 1976), 6.

[130] See K. Rajayyan, *Historiography: History in Theory and Method* (Madurai: Madurai Publishing House, 1976), 105-107. Hereafter cited as Rajayyan, *Historiography*.

[131] Cf. Rajayyan, *Historiography*, 100.

perspectives endeavour to explain the origins of our world and our place therein.

Ninthly, the principle of secularism advocates for the separation of religion and the state, whereas Christianity regards God as the supreme being at the centre of everything. Christian beliefs hold that history is not merely a narrative of human endeavours, but also a testament to God's perpetual reign and influence over the world.[132] As such, historical events are believed to be shaped not only by human action but also by God's divine plan and purpose.

Tenthly, the concept of secularism espouses the idea of a dichotomy between state and religion, whereas Christianity places God at the very centre of all things. It is contended that the Biblical vision of history is not an account of human beings alone, but rather a narrative of God's rule throughout history. This refers to the story of God's reign in history. Georges Florovsky's "The Predicament of the Christian Historian,"[133] offers insightful commentary on this topic. Florovsky posits that the Christian historian must acknowledge the role played by God in shaping historical events and should not view history solely through the lens of human being's activity. The Christian view of history revolves around the story of God's interaction with humanity and God's sovereignty over the world. Therefore, the dichotomy between state and religion that secularism promotes stands in stark contrast to Christianity's focus on placing God at the centre of all things. It is a unique interpretation of history that sees the world through a divine lens, rather than through the lens of human activity.

In evaluating secular and Christian history, it is possible to identify similarities and differences in their respective methods, sources, perspectives, and interpretations. Both fields share a commitment to rigorous analysis and critical assessment of primary

---

[132] See Georges Florovsky, "The Predicament of the Christian Historian," in *God, History and Historians: An Anthology of Modern Christian Views of History* ed. by McIntire (New York: Oxford University Press, 1977), 433.

[133] See Georges Florovsky, "The Predicament of the Christian Historian," in *God, History and Historians: An Anthology of Modern Christian Views of History* ed. by McIntire (New York: Oxford University Press, 1977), 433.

sources, although they diverge in their interpretive frameworks, teleological viewpoints, and historiographical traditions. Secular history adopts an objective and empirical approach, emphasizing the factual and evidential basis of historical events. By contrast, Christian history frequently incorporates theological perspectives, seeking to understand the interplay between faith practices and historical occurrences. These divergent approaches lead to disparate views regarding the meaning and significance of events. Additionally, secular, and Christian history diverge in their teleological outlooks, or their respective beliefs regarding the ultimate purpose or direction of history. Secular historians may view history as a sequence of random events, lacking any predetermined purpose. On the other hand, Christian historians often interpret history as a component of a divine plan or providential design. Lastly, these fields possess distinct historiographical traditions that have evolved over time. Secular history has been moulded by Enlightenment philosophy and a focus on rationality, while Christian history has been influenced by biblical scholarship and theological discourse. Recognizing these variations is fundamental to understanding the intersection of faith practices and historical inquiry. By doing so, we can gain a deeper comprehension of past events and their relevance to contemporary society.

Chapter 5

Approaches to History

The field of history comprises a wide range of techniques, procedures, and theoretical frameworks that historians employ to investigate and interpret the past. These techniques offer multiple perspectives from which historical phenomena can be examined, analysed, and contextualised. Historians must understand different perspectives in history to perform rigorous research, develop narratives, and comprehend the intricacies of human experience over time. This academic discourse delves into some of the most important approaches to history, emphasising their traits, methodology, and contributions to historical studies.

5.1. Hermeneutic Approaches to History

This approach focuses on the meaning of the actions and intentions of historical individuals rather than historical wholes. This tradition derives from the tradition of scholarly Biblical interpretation. Hermeneutic scholars emphasized the linguistic and symbolic core of human interactions and maintained that the techniques that had been developed to interpret texts could also be employed to interpret symbolic human actions and products.[134]

[134] See Daniel Little, "Philosophy of History," The Stanford Encyclopedia of Philosophy (Winter 2020 Edition), Edward N. Zalta (ed.), URL = https://plato.stanford.edu/archives/win2020/entries/history/ (5 Sep. 2023). Hereafter cited as Little, "Philosophy of History."

This method invites the thinker to engage in an active construction of the meanings and intentions of the actors from their point of view. This line of interpretation of human history found expression in the twentieth-century philosophical writings of Heidegger, Gadamer, Ricoeur, and Foucault. This tradition approaches the philosophy of history from the perspective of meaning and language. It argues that historical knowledge depends upon the interpretation of meaningful human actions and practices. Historians should probe historical events and actions to discover the interconnections of meaning and symbolic interaction[135] that the actions of human beings have created.

The hermeneutic tradition took an important new turn in the mid-twentieth century, as philosophers attempted to make sense of modern historical developments including war, racism, and the Holocaust. Narratives of progress were no longer compelling, following the terrible events of the first half of the twentieth century. The focus of this approach might be labelled "history as a remembrance." Contributors to this strand of thought emerged from twentieth-century European philosophy, including existentialism and Marxism, and were influenced by the search for meaning in the Holocaust. Paul Ricoeur draws out the parallels between personal memory, cultural memory, and history. Dominick LaCapra brings the tools of interpretation theory and critical theory to bear on his treatment of the representation of the trauma of the Holocaust. Others emphasize the role that folk histories play in the construction and interpretation of "our" past. This is a theme that has been taken up by contemporary historians, for example, by Michael Kammen in his treatment of public remembrance of the American Civil War. Memory and the representation of the past play a key role in the formation of racial and national identities; numerous twentieth-century philosophers have noted the degree of subjectivity and construction that are inherent in the national memories represented in a group's telling of its history.[136]

---

[135] See Little, "Philosophy of History."

[136] See Little, "Philosophy of History."

Collingwood focuses on the question of how to specify the content of history. He argues that history is constituted by human actions. Actions are the result of intentional deliberation and choice; so, historians can explain historical processes "from within" as a reconstruction of the thought processes of the agents who bring them about. He presents the idea of re-enactment as a solution to the problem of knowledge of the past from the point of view of the present. The past is accessible to historians in the present because it is open to them to re-enact important historical moments[137] through imaginative reconstruction of the actors' states of mind and intentions.

5.1.1. Methods and Practices

5.1.1.1. Contextual Analysis

Hermeneutical historians are scholars who specialize in analysing historical writings and artefacts through a socio-cultural, political, and intellectual lens. Their objective is to reconstruct the worldviews, values, and beliefs of historical actors by considering the context in which these documents and artefacts were created. The aim is to gain insights into how people in the past thought about the world around them and how they acted upon those beliefs. Hermeneutical historians conduct meticulous analyses of historical texts and artefacts to provide a better understanding of our collective past and its influence on the present. Through their analyses, hermeneutical historians explore the cultural, social, and political factors that shaped the creators of these historical documents. By examining the context in which these documents were created, they attempt to gain a deeper understanding of the values and beliefs of the historical actors. This approach is based on the premise that historical actors are not neutral observers of their surroundings, but rather active participants in shaping their environment.

In summary, hermeneutical historians provide valuable insights into the past by examining historical writings and artefacts in their socio-cultural, political, and intellectual contexts. Their

[137] See Little, "Philosophy of History."

work helps us to better understand the worldviews of historical actors and how these worldviews have influenced the present.

5.1.1.2. Interpretative Frameworks

Historians employ hermeneutical theory to elucidate the intricate meanings and significance embedded within historical materials. To this end, they employ interpretative frameworks, such as the horizon of understanding, fusion of horizons, and historical consciousness. By utilizing these frameworks, historians can effectively explore the context and background of events, as well as connect them to broader historical narratives. This approach allows for a comprehensive and nuanced understanding of the past, thereby facilitating the communication of its relevance to contemporary audiences. Through the application of these analytical tools, historians can effectively bring the past to life and contextualize it within the present.

5.1.1.3. Dialogue and Interpretation

Hermeneutical historians engage in a complex and dynamic process of interpreting historical events and texts, employing critical reflection, empathy, and reflexivity to acknowledge the diversity of views and perspectives. They approach the past with an open mind and strive to overcome biases, assumptions, and cultural contexts through rigorous analysis and reflection. Hermeneutical historians participate in a dialectical process of interpretation that enriches our understanding of the past and provides valuable insights into the human experience. This process involves a constant interaction between the historian and the historical subject, as well as a critical assessment of the historical evidence, including its context, provenance, and reliability. By engaging in this process, hermeneutical historians contribute to the advancement of historical knowledge and the development of new interpretive frameworks, revealing new dimensions of meaning and understanding that expand our horizons and deepen our appreciation of the past.

5.2. Social History

The field of social history is a scholarly discipline that concerns itself with the lives and experiences of people in the past. It focuses on the exploration of daily life, social structures, and cultural practices in various historical periods. The discipline seeks to explain how ordinary individuals lived, worked, and interacted with one another, as well as how their lives were shaped by broader social, economic, and political forces. Additionally, social history places a special emphasis on the experiences of marginalized groups such as women, minorities, and the working class, as well as social movements and struggles for social justice. A thorough understanding of social history enables us to examine the roots of current social issues and inequalities, providing insights that can help us to address contemporary societal challenges.

5.2.1. Characteristics

Social historians study class, gender, racism, ethnicity, and religion to better understand how people lived, interacted, and participated in historical events.

5.2.2. Methodologies

Social historians use a variety of materials, such as diaries, letters, oral histories, and material culture, to recreate social phenomena and analyse behavioural patterns. Social history also expands our comprehension of historical players beyond political elites, focusing light on the lives of common people and marginalised populations.

5.3. Cultural History

5.3.1. Definition

Cultural history is the study of the beliefs, values, symbols, and manifestations that have shaped societies' cultural identities throughout history. Cultural historians study cultural artefacts, literature, art, and popular culture to understand better how meanings and identities were produced, negotiated, and challenged.

The field of cultural history has been an object of study for more than two centuries. Its origins can be traced back to the Renaissance era, particularly in the fields of literature and philosophy. During this time, culture was associated with the growth of literary works, philosophical eloquence, law, arts, and sciences.[138] These fruits were deemed necessary for the development of the human virtues required for civil societies. The term "culture" was employed by Francis Bacon, Thomas Hobbes, Samuel Pufendorf, Gottfried Wilhelm von Leibniz, Johannes F. Buddeus, Christian Thomasius, and others during the seventeenth century to refer to the cultivation of the soul, mind, intellect, or reason. For example, Leibniz rendered it into the vernacular as "Cultur," or "Kultur."[139] The language was later transferred from an individual to a community as a means of identifying levels of civilization and assessing which citizens may be considered savage and which developed (advanced). Buddeus defined developed or advanced as morality, sociability, and the evolution from an animal state. The first inquiry concerned the roots of humanity's culture and manners and its emergence from a primaeval condition. In 1774, Jean-Bernard Mérian described primitive savages as a group of predators and navigators, devoid of civilization, legislation, or skills. Therefore, "culture," along with its counterpart, "barbarism," embodies Europeans' judgments of their own and other societies, both in the past and present. "Cultural history" emerged as an expression and notion during the late eighteenth century, as "culture" replaced previous analogues, such as "spirit" (men, esprit, Geist, etc.), which shifted from personal psychology to group mindset,[140] and literature, which pointed to all written remains of human cultural accomplishment.

5.3.2. Methodologies

Cultural historians examine cultural manifestations and behaviours using multidisciplinary methodologies that include anthropology,

---

[138] See "Cultural History," http://www.encyclopedia.com/history/dictionaries-thesauruses-pictures-and-press-releases/cultural-history (6 Apr. 2024), 1. Hereafter cited as "Cultural History."

[139] See "Cultural History," 1.

[140] See "Cultural History," 2.

literary theory, and visual studies. Cultural history contributes to our understanding of human experience by highlighting the role of cultural symbols, rituals, and traditions in forming historical awareness.

5.4. A History of Politics

Political history is the study of power, governance, institutions, and prior political movements. Political historians investigate the acts, decisions, and policies of political leaders, as well as the processes of state formation, diplomacy, conflict, and revolution.

5.4.1. Methodologies

Political historians employ a variety of methodologies to reconstruct political processes and analyse power dynamics. This involves extensive archival research, examination of official records, and application of political theory. Through these methods, political historians aim to gain a comprehensive understanding of political landscapes and the individuals who have shaped them. This enables them to shed light on complex interactions and power struggles that have influenced historical events. The work of political historians is of great importance in understanding the evolution of political systems and structures. Their analyses provide insights into how power is wielded, negotiated, and contested in different contexts. By examining political processes and power dynamics, political historians contribute to a deeper understanding of the forces that have shaped societies, governments, and institutions. Overall, the methodologies employed by political historians are essential for comprehending the complexities of political systems and power structures. Through their meticulous research and analysis, political historians provide valuable insights into the workings of politics and the individuals who have shaped it.

5.4.2. Contributions

An in-depth analysis of political history can reveal critical insights into the fundamental structures and dynamics of political systems, the nature of power struggles, and the critical role of ideology in shaping historical events. By examining historical events and movements in detail, we can gain a deeper understanding of the social, economic, and cultural forces that have influenced our world and make more informed decisions about our future direction. Therefore, it is essential to study political history in a business or academic setting to develop expertise in political systems, power dynamics, and ideological influences. This knowledge can help professionals and scholars make informed decisions and contribute meaningfully to society.

5.5. Digital History

The utilization of digital tools by historians has resulted in a profound transformation of the profession beyond mere practical and administrative gains. In the new millennium, computers and the internet have revolutionized historians' investigative methodologies, leading to the emergence of a novel internet-based history.[141] Digital history encompasses a range of initiatives that include the digitization of archives, libraries, and museums, computer-assisted research, web-based teaching, and the sharing of knowledge with the public regarding the past.[142] Additionally, it involves research into the history of digital, computers, and electronic devices.

However, digital data and metadata present new challenges for historians, necessitating a transition towards digital source criticism. It has become essential for historians to analyse all the available data, resulting in more systematic analysis. Digitization enables historians to analyse all available data instead of merely selectively sampling it. Conducting electronic historical investigations is generally more time-intensive and may require more deliberate methodological decisions than conventional historical methodology.[143] Digital history studies rely heavily on data selection, generation, cleaning, and filtering, in addition to algorithms, to produce accurate results.

---

[141] See M. Fridlund, M. Oiva, & P. Paju (Eds.), *Digital Histories: Emergent Approaches within the New Digital History* (Helsinki: Helsinki University Press, 2020), p. 3. Hereafter cited as Fridlund, *Digital Histories.*

[142] See Fridlund, *Digital Histories,* 12.

[143] See Fridlund, *Digital Histories,* 13.

Conclusion

Various historical approaches provide distinctive perspectives into the past's intricacies. From the hermeneutical method, which emphasises the process of interpretation and comprehension, to social, cultural, and political history, which investigates various facets of human experience, these approaches deepen historical knowledge and contribute to a more complete understanding of the past. Historians can create sophisticated narratives and interpretations of historical phenomena by combining multiple methodologies.

Chapter 6

History - A Science or an Art

The study of history has long been a subject of debate among scholars. While some argue that history is comparable to science in terms of its reliance on hypotheses and empirical evidence, others maintain that the two fields are fundamentally distinct. In this chapter, we will explore these differing perspectives and weigh the evidence for each. Whether you believe that history is a science or not, there is no denying its importance in shaping our understanding of the world. By examining the past, we gain valuable insights into the present and can better navigate the challenges of the future.

This chapter also delves into the concept of history as an art, exploring the multifaceted nature of historical inquiry and interpretation. The argument posits that history is not a mere science concerned with factual analysis but embodies qualities akin to an art form, characterized by narrative construction, interpretation, and creative expression. By examining the parallels between history and art, this chapter aims to illuminate the dynamic relationship between the discipline's empirical foundations and its imaginative dimensions. Moreover, this analysis underscores the importance of recognizing the nuanced and complex nature of historical inquiry, which involves a blend of objective analysis of factual data and subjective interpretation. Ultimately, this chapter calls for a re-evaluation of the traditional dichotomy between "science" and "art" in historical research and encourages scholars to embrace the creative and imaginative elements of the discipline.

6.1. History as a Science

It is debatable whether history belongs in the category of science. Modern historiography assumes that history is a science based on the historian's independent perspective as a scientific observer. Whether history is an art or a science is irrelevant, in G. R. Elton's opinion. Both apply.[144] However, not all historians agree with this premise.

History of the study of history cannot, in Durant's view, be a science. "It can only be an industry, an art, and a philosophy."[145] Another viewpoint, one that adopts a providential interpretation of history, is held by a conservative group. Gustavo Gutierrez's attempt to condense all human history into one single entity – God's salvific history - might have given rise to this viewpoint. It is challenging for G. M. Trevelyan, A. L. Rawse, Cohen, and others to refer to history as a science.[146]

However, most historians concur that history is a form of research or inquiry. The key point is that broadly speaking, it belongs to what we refer to as the sciences, which are intellectual processes in which we pose questions and seek to find answers.

Since scientists investigated the natural world and historians researched human beings, there was once thought to be a clear distinction between their fields of study. However, with the rise of environmental history and ecology, the distinctions have become blurred. The issue of methodology has long been at the centre of contention.

According to conventional wisdom, science works by creating hypotheses and then testing them, primarily through experiments. Scientists are objective observers who seek to understand the

---

[144] G. R. Elton, *The Practice of History* (Glasgow: William Collin's Sons and Co. Ltd., 1979), 16.

[145] Durant, *The Lessons*, 12.

[146] See Vanlalchhuanawma, "The Main Issues in Modern Historiography," unpublished paper, 5-7. Hereafter cited as Vanlalchhuanawma, "The Main Issues."

principles governing the physical world.[147] By understanding these laws, scientists may not only explain events that have already occurred but also make reliable forecasts.

From this, some historians have concluded that, while history is not the same as the natural sciences, it is sufficiently comparable to qualify as a science and, possibly, should be made more like one. Making assumptions and putting them to the test against the data is how history also moves forward.[148] Of course, historians also try to be always impartial and unbiased, just like the scientist.

The pursuit of truth is the common objective of history and science. History seeks to reveal the reality of the past, reconstructing the past exactly as it had actually occurred, and holding up a mirror to the past so that its genuine picture is mirrored whereas science is structured information and data for revealing the truths[149] underlying phenomena.

Since historical knowledge is generated from a critical analysis of the source material and is confirmed by additional referencing of the sources, it is not completely intuitive.[150] However, some content that a historian's explanations are not subject to the same level of scientific validation as physicists' claims are.

E. H. Carr answers those sceptics. According to his theory, scientists make discoveries and learn new things by formulating hypotheses rather than by creating precise, all-encompassing laws that pave the way for future research.[151] The primary scientific method literature by two American philosophers defines science as having a cyclical process. It is said that they use empirical data to support their claims about principles and that they choose, examine, and interpret this data following their principles. It would be better to use the word reciprocal rather than circular because the outcome is to go forward to new discoveries through a process of interaction

---

[147] See Morley, *Writing Ancient History*, 41.

[148] Cf. Morley, *Writing Ancient History*, 42.

[149] K. L. Khurana, *Concepts and Methods of Historiography*, 8th ed. (Agra: Laxmi Narain Agarwal, 2017), 35. Hereafter cited as Khurana, *Concepts and Methods.*

[150] See Webster, *An Introduction*, 27.

[151] See Carr, *What Is History?* 58.

between theories and facts, between theory and practice.[152] The position of the theories employed by the historian during his or her investigation appears to be very comparable to that of the theories employed by the scientist.

According to Arthur Warwick, experts might be heard urging the reform of scientific principles.[153] Professor Fred Hoyle confronted the Royal Astronomical Society in October 1968 with the need for fundamentally altering the laws of physics. Only then, Fred Hoyle claimed, would it be feasible to explain the absurdities of the cosmos. In the natural sciences, Warwick argues, there are no absolutes. Therefore, historians should not always reveal themselves as wholly unscientific when they are unable to provide definitive evidence[154] for their interpretation of historical events.

6.2. History as an Art

The study of history is a discipline that encompasses the investigation and analysis of past events, individuals, and cultures. It has traditionally been viewed as a social science that requires meticulous research, critical analysis, and the synthesis of evidence to develop historical narratives. However, beyond the realm of scientific inquiry, there exists a rich tapestry of imagination, interpretation, and storytelling that connects history and the domain of art. This section seeks to delve into the concept of history as an art form, emphasizing the interplay between scientific rigour and creative expression in historical studies.

6.2.1. The Narrative Paradigm

Even though one can also reason that history is art, it cannot be categorized as art in the same way that music, painting, and culture are. These artists use a different kind of faculty and concept in their

---

[152] As cited by M. R. Cohen, Ernest Nagel, An Introduction to Logic And Scientific Method (London: Routledge and Kegan Paul Ltd, 1934), 596.

[153] See Arthur Marwick, *The Nature of History*, 4th ed. (London: Macmillan Press Ltd, 1979), 99. Hereafter cited as Marwick, *The Nature.*

[154] See Marwick, *The Nature*, 99.

works than what the historian needs.[155] The historian must exercise artistic creativity and interpretive competence to give a new meaning to historical records. He or she is an artist in this sense because the orderly arrangement of elements produced by his or her artistic activity creates a relevant order.

Historians, like artists, create stories that connect diverse events, people, and cultural contexts to form compelling and unified narratives. Historians influence the shapes of these narratives by selecting and interpreting data and imparting interpretive frameworks, views, and biases. In this regard, the history technique is like the storytelling strategies used in literature, film, and other artistic genres, with an emphasis on narrative structure, character development, and thematic resonance.

Bridging the gaps between historical facts, as done by the historian, highlights the artistic elements of history as a profession. The historian's need to infer a personal narrative and piece together evidence to shape a new version of history is an unavoidable aspect of the historical writing process. History would be extremely difficult to comprehend without this narrative structure.[156] At this time, it is obvious that history has begun to resemble an artistic profession.

6.2.2. Interpretive Flexibility

Historical scholarship highly values interpretive flexibility, which allows for the coexistence of multiple perspectives and opposing narratives. The analysis of historical events and personalities, like works of art, can vary significantly depending on the historian's theoretical orientation, cultural background, and ideological beliefs. This interpretive multiplicity plays a crucial role in improving historical discourse by fostering debate, contemplation, and critical engagement with the past. Additionally, it emphasizes the subjective aspect of historical investigations, reminding us that historical information is always provisional and dependent on the viewpoints of those who interpret it.

---

[155] Vanlalchhuanawma, "The Main Issues," 7.

[156] See "History as Art or Science" https//:owlcation.com/humanities/History-Art-or-Science (17 July 2023).

Interpretive flexibility in historical scholarship allows for the consideration of diverse viewpoints, which enhances the rigour of historical discourse. It is important to acknowledge the subjective nature of historical inquiry and to remain open to the possibility of multiple perspectives. By doing so, we can approach historical analysis with a critical eye and engage in productive discussions that advance our understanding of the past.

6.2.3. Creative Expression

The discipline of history encompasses not only empirical investigation and documentation but also creative expression that goes beyond factual reconstruction. Historians employ a variety of imaginative tactics, including literary devices, visual representations, and rhetorical flourishes, to revive past events and captivate their audience. They employ the art of storytelling, utilizing language to bring history to life, promoting empathy, comprehension, and a sense of connection among their readers. In adopting this approach, history serves not only as a repository of facts but also as a medium for artistic appreciation and creative discovery.

6.3. History as a Fusion of Science and Art - Investigating the Dynamic Interplay of Empirical Rigour and Creative Interpretation

History, as a synthesis of science and art, relies on the dynamic interaction between empirical rigour and creative interpretation. While scientific approaches provide the framework for historical research, artistic expression gives history vitality, meaning, and human importance. The friction between objectivity and subjectivity, fact, and interpretation, creates a dialectical interaction that enriches historical knowledge and broadens our understanding of the past. Historians may negotiate the complexity of history with nuance, insight, and empathy by incorporating both scientific analytical tools and artistic imaginative capacities, transcending disciplinary boundaries to offer varied perspectives on the human condition.

We may reasonably argue that history is a scientific and art-based academic discipline. Despite historical methodology's past attempts to be basically scientific or essentially artistic, the true image is more like a complicated interaction between the two. Because of this, historians are wary of words and definitions that are extremely specific, as Hughes points out:

> Historians are by nature wary of precise definition; they hate to be confined within tight terminological boundaries, and they are ever alert to the fallacy of misplaced concreteness; they much prefer to write ordinary words in their common-sense usage and then let the reader little by little become aware of how these words have subtly changed their significance through time.[157]

Hughes has made a strong argument in favour of a more inclusive viewpoint that views both science and art as languages:[158]

> The two processes, that of science and that of art are not very different. Both science and art form the centuries a human language by which we can speak about the more remote part of reality, and the coherent sets of concepts as well as the different styles of art are different words or groups of words in this language.

The hard data evidence that historians investigate includes papers, artefacts, testimony, various written records, and more. However, they must evaluate this data and present it in a way that is comprehensible and intelligible. Marius and Page expertly highlight this fundamental element of the historian's efforts:

> Solving such puzzles of history involves both science and art. Science is a synonym for knowledge. But knowledge of what? History includes data evidence, the names of people and places, when things happened, where they happened, and bits of information gathered from many

[157] H. Stuart Hughes, *History as Art and as Science: Twin Vistas on the Past* (New York: Harper and Row, 1964), 3. Hereafter cited as Hughes, *History.*

[158] Hughes, *History,* 2.

> sources. It also includes interpretations of historians and others in the past who have written on the topic that the writer decided to treat in an essay. The art of history lies in combining fact and interpretation to tell a story about the past…[159]

To summarise, history as an integration of science and art represents the combination of empirical rigour and artistic interpretation, providing a diverse prism through which to understand the past. Historians may reveal the complexity of human experience, expose the contours of collective memory, and deepen our understanding of the world we live in by respecting the dynamic interplay between these two worlds. Recognising history's ability to connect scientific investigation and artistic expression confirms its long-term importance as a scholarly subject and a cultural endeavour, inviting us to interact with the past in all its complexity, plurality, and intricacy.

---

[159] Richard Marius and Melvin E. Page, *A Short Guide to Writing About History*, 7th ed. (New York: Pearson Education Inc, 2010), 3.

Chapter 7

Presentation of Historical Materials

The study of history is captivating and offers several presentation styles, each tailored to suit the context, objective, and audience. Among the popular techniques used for presenting history are the narrative, analytical, and chronological approaches. The narrative approach involves retelling events in a story format, while the analytical approach scrutinizes and interprets historical events and their relevance. The chronological approach, however, presents historical events in chronological order to provide a sequential comprehension of the past. These techniques have their distinct advantages and play a crucial role in helping us attain an all-encompassing understanding of history.

7.1. Narrative Presentation

7.1.1. Definition

Narrative presentation tells a story or describes events in a chronological and sequential format. It is intended to create a clear and interesting story that enables the audience to understand and interpret past events. Narrative structures help shape our perception of a period and our interpretation of the evidence.[160] Narrative history might seem alarmingly like fiction.

[160] See Neville Morley, *Writing Ancient History* (London: Bloomsbury, 2002), 110.

The primary goal of narratives is to serve as a historical account of past events and significant occurrences in people's lives. These narratives may provide historical context and explain why certain circumstances occurred.[161] Although narrative tales have been a fundamental aspect of historical literature for many years, they are now considered an immature and inferior type of history. They are often criticized for being superficial and focusing on short-term events instead of exploring the institutions that influenced the course of events. Moreover, they present a deceptive and politically problematic view of the past, primarily dominated by upper-class political and military activity. Despite this, narratives serve as a critical foundation for historical interpretation and cannot be avoided entirely.

7.1.2. Characteristics

Narrative history typically presents events chronologically, creating a timeline of historical developments. It emphasizes the actions, motivations, and impact of major persons on historical events. This type of history focuses on storytelling to engage audiences and immerse them in historical events. However, historians' biases, viewpoints, and interpretations shape how events are portrayed. In ancient and medieval times, historians and scholars were often closely linked with the royal court, and what they wrote was essentially flattery for their patron. As a result, scholars mixed facts and fiction in such a way that it has become difficult for modern scholars to distinguish between them.

7.1.3. Advantages

Narrative history is captivating for mass audiences, making history more relatable and intelligible. It contextualizes historical events, providing a rich understanding of the past. Focusing on individuals and personal stories can increase empathy and emotional resonance, making history more memorable.

---

[161] See Neville Morley, *Writing Ancient History* (London: Bloomsbury, 2002), 110.

7.2. Analytical Presentation

7.2.1. Definition

Analytical presentation of history involves a comprehensive investigation and interpretation of historical events, trends, causes, and outcomes. It aims to analyze and interpret the past using critical inquiry and theoretical frameworks. Analytical history follows the tone and approach of rigorous, factual scientific studies such as sociology.[162] It requires historical vision, literary aptitude, and standard historical analysis skills.

7.2.2. Characteristics

Analytical history investigates the fundamental causes, patterns, and implications of historical events, going beyond simple description. It incorporates various methodologies, including theories, methods, and views from sociology, economics, and political science. Evidence evaluation involves assessing historical sources for dependability, biases, and limitations to build strong arguments and interpretations. Analytical history explores topics, concepts, and historical patterns instead of following a strict chronological sequence.

7.2.3. Advantages

Analytical history provides a deeper understanding of historical processes, structures, and dynamics, facilitating critical thinking and analysis. Contextualizing historical events allows for a more nuanced understanding by considering their social, political, and cultural contexts. Additionally, it identifies historical patterns, cycles, and trends, providing insights into human behaviour and societal change.

7.3. Chronological Presentation

7.3.1. Definition

When it comes to understanding history, arranging events in a strict chronological order can be incredibly helpful. This approach

---

[162] See Neville Morley, *Writing Ancient History* (London: Bloomsbury, 2002), 110.

emphasizes the sequence of past events without getting bogged down in interpretation or narrative. By following a chronological presentation, we can gain a clearer and more accurate understanding of how things unfolded in the past.

7.3.2. Characteristics

This type of presentation presents events chronologically, providing a clear timeline of historical developments. It arranges events based on factual correctness and objectivity, avoiding subjective interpretations. It provides comprehensive coverage by offering an overview of historical periods, movements, or subjects within a certain period. It suggests a reference point by providing a framework for future study, interpretation, or narrative development.

7.3.3. Advantages

The chronological presentation of history provides a clear and structured framework for understanding historical events, allowing for easy comprehension and reference. It also provides the foundation for historical scholarship - a solid foundation for analysis, interpretation, and storytelling. It gives a chronological perspective by identifying causality and continuity between historical events.

Finally, narrative, analytical, and chronological presentations of history each provide distinct viewpoints and serve different functions in comprehending the past. While narrative presentations captivate viewers with stories, analytical presentations go further into interpretation and analysis, and chronological presentations provide a formal framework for organizing historical events. A thorough understanding of history frequently includes combining different techniques and leveraging their unique strengths to create a nuanced and perceptive depiction of the past.

Chapter 8

Problems of Objectivity, Subjectivity, and Bias

When we present a case or write a historical account, it is common to face the challenge of subjectivity and bias. Even when we try to remain objective, it is difficult to avoid personal opinions and beliefs from creeping in. That can lead to a lack of credibility and accuracy in our writing. The importance of achieving objectivity in writing cannot be overstated. It requires an understanding of the different perspectives and interpretations of a situation, as well as the ability to present all sides of the story fairly and rationally. In this chapter, we delve into the problem of objectivity, subjectivity, and bias. We explore the different ways in which these factors can influence our writing and provide practical tips and strategies to help mitigate their impact.

8.1. Definition of Objectivity

Academic objectivity in research is the process of conducting scholarly studies free of bias, personal viewpoints, and preconceived assumptions. Objectivity is a vital concept in any field of study, as it allows for a clear and unbiased examination of the subject matter. It is a connection between the inquisitive individual and the external object of study, which requires an emphasis on the object itself rather than on personal or cultural biases.[163] Objectivity is the result of a collaborative effort by a group of experts who scrutinize the objects they investigate and engage in critical discourse with each other.

To provide accurate and reliable results, historians and social scientists must remain impartial and unbiased in their analysis. Objectivity demands that they remain free from any personal prejudices or inclinations that could influence their findings. It enables them to collect and analyse data with utmost accuracy, without any tampering or alterations. This approach ensures that their findings are legitimate and reflect the truth, irrespective of any personal feelings, imagination, or thoughts.[164] Objectivity is a vital trait that enables researchers to achieve realism and uphold the integrity of their work.

The truth that emerges from this process, whether expressed in theory, generalisations, or explanations, is comprehensive and cohesive. It is worth noting that achieving complete objectivity is a challenging task, as it requires individuals to put aside their personal biases and beliefs.[165] However, it is crucial to strive towards objectivity, as it provides a solid foundation for the development of knowledge. In the field of history, for example, accredited scholars recognise the importance of objectivity in uncovering the truth about the past.

In the second half of the twentieth century, there were probably only a small number of accredited historical scholars who believed that they were entirely unbiased[166] and that the information they uncovered through their research was the truth in its entirety. While complete objectivity may be difficult to achieve, it is a goal worth pursuing.

---

[163] See John C. B. Webster, *Studying History,* reprinted (Delhi: Macmillan, 2006), 30. Hereafter cited as Webster, *Studying History.*

[164] Cf. Sabnam, "What does it mean to have objectivity?" https://www.sociologygroup.com/objectivity.

[165] See Webster, *Studying History*, 30.

[166] See Webster, *Studying History*, 25.

8.1.1. Key Components of Academic Objectivity

8.1.1.1. Impartiality

Researchers aim to be objective by eliminating favouritism or prejudices towards any certain outcome. They tackle an investigation question with a willingness to listen and critically evaluate evidence, regardless of personal ideas or preferences.

8.1.1.2. Transparency

For research to be objective, the methodology, data gathering, and analysis procedures must be transparent. Researchers should fully describe their processes, assumptions, and constraints so that others can determine the validity and dependability of their findings.

8.1.1.3. Systematic Inquiry

Academic objectivity comprises a methodical method of inquiry, in which scholars follow established techniques and protocols for data collection and analysis. This systematic technique minimises the impact of individual inclinations on the investigative procedure.

8.1.1.4. Critical Thinking

Critical thinking and scepticism are essential components to study objectivity. Before reaching any conclusions, researchers critically assess the proof offered, examine suppositions, and weigh alternate possibilities. They are willing to revise their hypotheses in the face of fresh facts or insights.

8.1.1.5. Peer Review

The method of peer review reinforces academic objectivity by evaluating the efficacy and authenticity of the investigation before it is published. Peer review ensures that research meets academic standards and adds to the common understanding in a trustworthy and reliable way.

8.2. Subjectivity

8.2.1. Definition of Subjectivity

Subjectivity includes thoughts, beliefs, and preferences that shape an individual's identity. It opposes objectivity, which seeks impartiality and separation. Ignoring subjectivity in qualitative research would be equivalent to missing an important element of understanding.[167]

Subjectivity, defined as a person's distinctive viewpoint or perspective on real life, is a fundamental component of human experience. Subjectivity, which is founded on the subjective character of awareness, refers to a wide range of phenomena, including personal thoughts and emotions, as well as accepted norms and societal structures.

One may define subjectivity as the bias or viewpoint that is present in human thought and perception. Unlike objectivity, which seeks impartiality and neutrality, subjectivity recognises the inevitable impact caused by one's own experiences, values, and social context on one's personal views. In philosophy, subjectivity is frequently contrasted with objectivity, representing the conflict between subjective truths and objective reality. While objectivity seeks consistency and neutrality, subjectivity values the variety of individual experiences and perceptions.

In conclusion, subjectivity is a component of human cognition and communication, permeating all aspects of human experience. Recognising the inherent subjectivity of perception and interpretation allows us to develop more awareness, empathy, and reflexivity in our interactions with others and the environment surrounding us. Furthermore, by accepting subjectivity as an inherent component of the human experience, we can promote a more inclusive and pluralistic vision of reality, overcoming the constraints of restricted perspectives and biases. Thus, the study of subjectivity provides crucial insights into the nature of consciousness, knowledge, and social interaction, so, enriching our grasp of the intricacies of human experience.

---

[167] See Elizabeth M. Pope, "Subjectivity in Educational Research," https://www.westga.edu/academics/research/vrc/assets/docs/subjectivity-reflexivity-notes.pdf (9 Apr. 2024).

Methodologists advocate several additional actions to guarantee that one uses subjectivity correctly. Among these, we may observe:[168]

a) Sending the investigation findings to colleagues and other professionals in the subject or comparing the results with earlier studies.
b) Group data analysis for consensus.
c) Validity and reliability measures, including triangulation.
d) Present objective text-based analysis results before subjective analysis.
e) Making use of respondents throughout the research process.

8.3. Bias

8.3.1. Definition of Bias

Bias is the inclination to form opinions about something, either positively or negatively.[169] Bias can be seen throughout history.[170] To cite an example, many people of high-caste or high-class origins tend to regard people of lower-caste or lower-class backgrounds as fundamentally inferior and to regard only those from their own group as equals. This is part of the human condition. Our social context and prior experience determine the type of prejudice we have.[171]

Bias can be of two kinds: explanation bias and hindsight prejudice. Explanation bias is the tendency of human beings to assign greater certainty to historical causality than the evidence warrants. That bias is inextricably tied to the concepts of uncertainty and ignorance, as it refers to their undervaluing in

---

[168] See Martin Drapeau, "Subjectivity in Research: Why Not? But…" *TQR* 7Q/3 (9.1.2002).

[169] See Hunter P. Mabry, *A Manual for Researchers and Writers,* 2nd ed. (Bangalore: BTESSC, 2011), 99. Hereafter cited as Mabry, *A Manual.*

[170] See Khurana, *Concepts and Methods*, 83.

[171] See Mabry, *A Manual*, 99.

historical analysis[172] and overvaluing of a single causal explanation for a given occurrence.

Hindsight bias is the tendency of individuals to overestimate in retrospect what they may have predicted in advance.[173] In other words, following a past occurrence, people tend to assume they were more certain of the outcome than they were, a phenomenon that psychologist Baruch Fischhoff dubbed "creeping determinism."[174] It refers to people's inclination to regard past occurrences as more foreseeable than they really were. The election of Donald Trump in 2016 serves as an illustration. While most Democrats easily confess, that they were taken aback by his victory, many more today (than at the time) claim to have had legitimate worries in the run-up to election day. However, hindsight bias informs us that these individuals now overestimate the problems they had at the time. This is because, in retrospect, people have a difficult time remembering how much they did not know at the time (i.e., their past uncertainty), and their knowledge of the outcome distorts their memory.[175]

8.3.2. Bias in History Teaching

History, like any other field, is susceptible to biases. Whether intentional or not, biases have long been present in historical

---

[172] See Aroop Mukharji and Richard Zeckhauser, "Bound to Happen: Explanation Bias in Historical Analysis," *Journal of Applied History* 1(1), 2019, https://brill.com/view/journals/joah/joah-overview.xml (21 Sept. 2023).

[173] See: Baruch Fischhoff, "Hindsight not Equal to Foresight: the Effect of Outcome Knowledge on Judgment Under Uncertainty," *Journal of Experimental Psychology: Human Perception and Performance*, Vol. 1 (1975), pp. 288-299; and Baruch Fischhoff, "For Those Condemned to Study the Past: Heuristics and Biases in Hindsight," in Daniel Kahneman, Paul Slovic, and Amos Tversky, eds., *Judgment Under Uncertainty: Heuristics and Biases* (Cambridge, UK: Cambridge University Press, 1982), 335-351.

[174] See Aroop Mukharji and Richard Zeckhauser, "Bound to Happen: Explanation Bias in Historical Analysis," *Journal of Applied History* 1(1), 2019, https://brill.com/view/journals/joah/joah-overview.xml (21 Sept. 2023).

[175] See Aroop Mukharji and Richard Zeckhauser, "Bound to Happen: Explanation Bias in Historical Analysis," *Journal of Applied History* 1(1), 2019, https://brill.com/view/journals/joah/joah-overview.xml (21 Sept. 2023).

research, leading to prejudices developing, evolving, and even disappearing. The emergence of Eurocentrism during the 18th and 19th centuries is a prime example of how biases can amplify and become ingrained in history.[176] Despite attempts to turn history into an objective and empirical study, Western historians mainly disregarded aspects of history, such as class, gender, and race.

Until the emergence of social history in the 1960s and 1970s, Western historical narratives mainly focused on the military and political aspects of history, while cultural or social history was primarily written from the elites' viewpoint. The biased approach used in history writing extended to history teaching, with history textbooks often serving as tools to promote nationalism,[177] patriotism, and a positive account of national history.

However, Germany is leading the way in eliminating nationalistic narratives from history education, with its history curriculum emphasizing a transnational perspective that highlights the common European heritage, minimizes the concept of national pride, and promotes civil society based on democracy, human rights, and peace. Despite progress and increased attention to historically marginalized groups, bias remains a part of historical research.[178] It is crucial to acknowledge biases so that we can continue to challenge them and ensure that history is an accurate and inclusive representation of our past.

8.3.3. Tips to Avoid Bias

Researchers should consider whether a writer's own bias or predisposition has led to an overemphasis on evidence that supports their opinion. To some extent, prejudgments will always exist. Because researchers are rarely neutral investigators, they must be self-critical and capable of recognising and thoughtfully considering data,

---

[176] See "Historical Bias," https://www.boundless.com/world-history/textbooks/boundless-world-history-textbook/ (21 Sept. 2023). Hereafter cited as "Historical Bias."

[177] See "Historical Bias," 2.

[178] See "Historical Bias," 3.

evidence, or materials that contradict their preconceived notions,[179] allowing for the possibility of progress in understanding.

Knowing something about a writer's history can help you spot any bias. If evidence is supplied that contradicts the writer's bias, this helps to raise the possibility that the author's work is a reliable report.[180]

Do not be fooled by misleading information. Scrutinize how the author characterizes people or events, and watch out for language that may skew the truth. Keep an eye out for any significant points that the source may be overlooking. Fact-check everything. Make sure that the information presented is accurate and reliable.

8.4. Implications of Objectivity, Subjectivity, and Bias

The interplay between objectivity, subjectivity, and bias has significant implications for knowledge formation, social justice, and relationships. While objectivity is a guiding concept in scientific study and media, admitting subjectivity encourages reflexivity and empathy in comprehending other points of view. To reduce unjust treatment or discrimination, one must address bias through critical awareness, cultural competency, and systemic solutions. Furthermore, acknowledging the limitations of objectivity and the pervasiveness of prejudice helps improve ethical decision-making and social equality.

In retrospect, objectivity, subjectivity, and bias are key categories for negotiating the intricacies of human mental processes, understanding, and interaction. Subjectivity recognises the variety of people's experiences and views, whereas objectivity is a lofty target for impartial inquiry. However, prejudice is a pervasive impediment to obtaining objectivity, needing constant awareness and cognizance in scholarly endeavours. By seriously interacting with these ideas, researchers and scholars can promote a more serious and encompassing search for information, thereby improving debate, and understanding across disciplines and communities.

---

179 See Mabry, *A Manual,* 99.

180 See Mabry, *A Manual,* 100.

Chapter 9

Evaluation of Sources

Historians bear a significant responsibility in ensuring the reliability of the sources they utilize. To accomplish this, they must engage in two types of analysis: Internal and External Criticism.[181] These methods of critique are particularly relevant in academic, philosophical, artistic, and literary domains. External criticism involves evaluating a piece of writing or material based on factors that are not present within the work itself. This may include how audiences react to the project, the author's background and biography, the historical context, or the cultural background of the author. Internal criticism, on the other hand, aims to analyse the work itself. This includes a thorough examination of the language used, the topics covered, the structure employed, and the internal coherence of the piece. By engaging in both Internal and External criticism, historians can ensure that the sources they use are reliable and trustworthy. To evaluate the reliability of a source, it is important to engage in External criticism, which involves scrutinizing elements that are not intrinsic to the work. This may include analysing the audience's reaction to the material, examining the author's background and biography, or considering

[181] See K. N. Chitnis, *Research Methodology in History*, fourth ed. (New Delhi: Atlantic Publishers and Distributors Pvt. Ltd., 2023), 44. Hereafter cited as Chitnis, *Research Methodology*.

the historical and cultural context in which it was produced. By considering these external factors, historians can better understand the context in which the material was produced, as well as its potential biases and limitations.

In addition to External Criticism, Internal Criticism is also essential in evaluating the reliability of a source. This involves a close analysis of the work itself, including its language, structure, and internal consistency. By examining the work in detail, historians can better understand its meaning and value, as well as its potential limitations or inaccuracies.

9.1. External Criticism

The comprehension of works of literature or research documents necessitates an exploration of their original cultural and historical context. For example, the examination of Mahatma Gandhi's thought processes requires the consideration of the social and cultural milieu present in India before its independence. Similarly, feminist theology should be approached as a reflection of women's attempts to theologically reflect upon their particular setting,[182] rather than as the writings of colonial writers.

The process of scrutinizing texts involves the application of External Criticism, which entails locating the original manuscripts, identifying the authors, time and place of origin, and sources[183] from which they were derived.

Language is situational by nature and evolves over time. Old words lose their meaning, new words develop, and even terms from the same era might have distinct meanings to different people or groups. Research in any field is shaped by society and culture, hence scholars must exert effort in contextualizing their findings within the historical setting[184] in which they originated to ensure accuracy.

---

[182] Cf. Hunter P. Mabry, *A Manual for Researchers and Writers of Course Assignments, Theses, Dissertations, and Other Research Reports*, 2nd ed. (Bangalore: B.T.E.S.S.C., 2011), 88. Hereafter cited as Mabry, *A Manual.*

[183] See Chitnis, *Research Methodology*, 44.

[184] See Mabry, *A Manual*, 88.

The question of how unique a text is can be answered in one of the following ways. Firstly, the text may be the original manuscript in question, necessitating little further examination. Alternatively, it may be the only surviving duplicate of the original, requiring examination to determine its archetype. However, this can be challenging as the duplicate may be a forgery, either intentionally or otherwise.[185] In such cases, researchers must be familiar with the language and script of the era, as well as the unique meanings of technical terms as they were used at the time of the text's creation to identify any potential forgeries.

In other words, the comprehension of works of literature or research documents requires a consideration of their cultural and historical context. Additionally, researchers must be aware of how language evolves over time and contextualize their findings within the broader societal and cultural setting in which they originated. Finally, when examining texts, it is crucial to determine whether they are the original or a surviving duplicate,[186] and if the latter, to ascertain their authenticity.

The process of transcribing an original text can result in unintentional errors that alter the original meaning of the text. These errors may be attributed to incorrect assessments or unintentional slips by the transcribers. During the process of copying, transcribers may have attempted to rectify the text's grammar, leading to errors such as dittography, haplography, misreading, poor punctuation, word transposition, and sense misunderstanding. Therefore, examining different versions of the same content critically becomes a crucial step in determining the most trustworthy version of a lost or damaged text. Additional examinations such as palaeography, writing style, paper used, abbreviations, and historical antecedents can be used to identify the text closer to the archetype[187] and, therefore, more trustworthy.

Moreover, supporting claims with information gathered from as many different sources as possible is essential. Critical analysis

---

[185] See Chitnis, *Research Methodology*, 45.

[186] See Chitnis, *Research Methodology*, 45.

[187] See Chitnis, *Research Methodology*, 45-47.

of various materials helps to differentiate between convincing and insufficient proof.[188] It is feasible to distinguish between reliable and insufficient evidence by critically analysing materials from various sources.

9.2. Internal Criticism

Internal criticism aims to scrutinize the contents of the text from the inside out and identify any historical details that can be taken as accurate.[189] Positive Analysis/Criticism and Negative Analysis/Criticism are the two processes that make up Internal Criticism.

9.2.1. The Positive Analysis/Criticism

Positive analysis focuses on determining the author's meaning behind numerous comments stated in their publications, which helps decode the text's meaning by understanding the language of the era in which the text was written. Understanding the language of the era is necessary to comprehend the text's proper meaning,[190] especially when some words are no longer in use or have changed meaning significantly over time.

Determining authorship for contemporary published materials is typically not problematic. However, putting an author's name on a work has only gained popularity in the past 200 years. Therefore, claims of authorship cannot always be taken at face value. When authorship cannot be independently verified, inside proof such as primary concepts, often repeated phrases that appear in other works by the same author,[191] and the technique of writing can be considered.

9.2.2. The Negative Analysis/Criticism

Negative Analysis/Critique questions the sincerity of the writer and ascertains whether the author is biased. For instance, if the author belongs to a political party, statements about the party are typically

---

[188] See Mabry, *A Manual*, 88.

[189] See Chitnis, *Research Methodology*, 50.

[190] See Chitnis, *Research Methodology*, 50.

[191] See Mabry, *A Manual*, 91.

biased against other parties and beneficial to the author's party.[192] Similarly, remarks made by someone who belongs to a favoured group or clan are likely to exalt that family or clan while demeaning or neglecting other families.

Therefore, historians must engage in both internal and external criticism to ensure the reliability of the sources they use. Through these methods of analysis, they can better understand the context in which the material was produced and evaluate its potential biases and limitations. By conducting thorough evaluations of the sources they use, historians can ensure that their work is reliable, credible, and trustworthy.

---

[192] See Chitnis, *Research Methodology*, 52.

Chapter 10

Historiography

10.1. Meaning of Historiography

The Shorter Oxford English Dictionary on Historical Principles describes historiography as "the writing of history, written history or about written history."[193] Sean Lang defines it as the "study of the study of history" and adds it that it involves studying historians in terms of both what they have written and the times in which they wrote it.[194] According to the Oxford Advanced Learner's Dictionary, it is "the study of writing about history."[195] Merriamwebster.com, a renowned online dictionary defines it as "the writing of history, especially the writing of history based on the critical examination of sources, the selection of particulars from the authentic materials, and the synthesis of particulars into a narrative that will stand the test of critical methods or the principles, theory and history of historical

---

[193] "Historiography," *The Shorter Oxford English Dictionary on Historical Principles,* edited by C. T. Onions, 3rd ed. (Oxford: Clarendon Press, ny): 906.

[194] See Sean Lang, "The First Year Experience," in *History Skills – A Student's Handbook,* edited by Mary Abbott, 3rd ed. (London: Routledge, 2009), 13.

[195] "Historiography," in *Oxford Advanced Learner's Dictionary,* edited by Leonie Hey and Suzanne Holloway (United Kingdom: Oxford University Press, 2015): 744.

writing."[196] Historiography tells the story of the phases of the advancement or development of historical accounts and records in a row. It considers the evolution of the ideas and techniques associated with the writing of history and the changing attitudes toward the nature of history itself.[197] It comprises the learning of the progress of human beings' sense and logic in the past.

In a nutshell, historiography is a study of how history is written based on examination of sources and selection of facts as well as how the historian gives elucidation, interpretation, and analysis of his/her facts. It is the theory and method of historical scholarship. While history *per se* is a historian's restoration of the past, historiography is the record and account of historical thought. As V. V. Thomas fittingly said, historiography "is a study of the methodology of historical research and the skills of scrutinizing historical records. Often it is used in the sense of historical methodology. More often historiography means a study of perspectives."[198] Historiography, therefore, is a record of perspectives, contests, conflicts, and consequences of the past. It is the study of how historians perceive the past concerning the historical setting in which they wrote about it.

10.2. Why Do We Have a Range of Historiographies?

Historians have been divided into different camps[199] and their styles of writing are at variance from one to that of another. On closer inquiry, the variations basically meet at certain points due to inconsistencies and obscuration like history and sometimes of the historian himself/herself. Differences, agreement, overlapping, and harmony prevail. This fairly deserves our closer observation.

---

[196] "Definition of historiography," https://www.merriam-webster.com/dictionary/historiography (25 July 2018).

[197] Butterfield, "Historiography," *Dictionary of History of Ideas,* edited by Philip Paul Wiener, Vol. 2 (Minnesota: Scribner, 1973), 464.

[198] V. V. Thomas, *Dalit and Tribal Christians of India – Issues and Challenges* (Malapuram: Focus India Trust, 2014), 16. Hereafter cited as V. V. Thomas, *Dalit and Tribal Christians.*

[199] Such as positivists, conformists, relativists, determinists and the like.

The positivistic view of history maintains that the sources are all-important and that the truths or facts subsist independently of the historian. They believe that total objectivity is achievable in the writing of history and accordingly, they presume that history can be regarded as science. "First ascertain the facts," said the Positivists, "then draw your conclusions from them."[200] As already reflected in chapter 2 of this book, "What I want," said Mr. Gradgrind in *Hard Times,* "is facts…Facts alone are wanted in life."[201] They believe in the methods and truths of natural sciences and thus claim that history deals with certainty, authenticity, or reality. They argue that history exists outside of the discernment of the historian.[202] This view ignores the principle that facts are subjective and not objective.

With enthusiasm, historians set to work to determine as many facts as they could. That led to a gigantic enhancement of meticulous historical knowledge. The field of invention, discovery, and unearthing was never-ending and they asked nothing better than to investigate it.[203] In line with this, Marx and Hegel assumed that history observed the operation of real occurrences or facts. This led them to believe that a historian has the aptitude to find out the actuality of the course of action or historical process.[204] The problem, with this, is that simple discovering of facts for their own sake was substandard and unsatisfactory.

Historian-thinkers like Croce, Carl Becker and Collingwood came out to argue against the establishment of such an approach of neutrality, scientific, and objectivity. They rejected the idea of the existence of facts independent of the historian and gave great

---

[200] Carr, *What is History?* 9.

[201] Carr, *What is History?* 8.

[202] Cf. Sawmpuia, "Positivist View of History," http://puchistory.blogspot.com/2015/01/positivist-view-of-history.html (31 July 2018). Hereafter cited as Sawmpuia, "Positivist View of History."

[203] See R. G. Collingwood, *The Idea of History,* revised ed. (New Delhi: Oxford University Press, 2000), 127. Hereafter cited as Collingwood, *The Idea of History,* 128.

[204] See Norman F. Cantor and Richard I Schneider, *How to Study History* (Arlington Heights, Illinois: AHM Publishing Corporation, 1967), 256, 257. Hereafter cited as Norman F. Cantor and Richard I Schneider, *How to Study History.*

importance to "interpretation" in history writing.[205] Auguste Comte also proposed that historical facts must be employed as the raw material of something more important and more legitimately fascinating or appealing than themselves.[206] Process and causation could no longer be considered as understood in an objectified history itself. Relatively, they are to be recognized as a fraction of the historian's own beliefs and judgments, part of the decision-making that guided the historian in delivering the verdict on history. "Most history is guessing," declares Will Durant, "and the rest is prejudice."[207] R. G. Collingwood observes history as the product of a historian's "imaginative construction."[208] In the same vein, Carl Becker aggressively argued that "the facts of history do not exist for any historian till he [sic] creates them."[209] This is a more rational way of interpreting history and mostly is reasonable.

Historical facts are not given but constructed. The historian's own assessments were seen to be the determining factor of the truth that they used in making conclusions about the past. "Historical process was not an objectified reality: it was the act of thinking and writing itself. Historians did not discover history: they created it."[210] This tradition governed the end of nineteenth-century history writing and even in the twentieth century most of the historians followed this trend. Twentieth-century relativism, therefore, argues that every historian picks, condemns and passes judgment on history according to his/her individual assessment.

In the pre-modern world, the public feasted their eyes on learned and knowledgeable persons for reliable answers to their questions. The modern world, on the other hand, contested the rights of those who have authority on certain subjects. The obligation was made in the search for fact, reality, and truth, "which turned into

---

[205] Sawmpuia, "Positivist View of History," 1.

[206] See Collingwood, *The Idea of History,* 128.

[207] Will and Ariel Durant, *The Lessons of History* (Bombay: Mohan Punjabi Hans Publishers, 1977), 12.

[208] F. Cantor and Richard I Schneider, *How to Study History*, 258.

[209] As cited by Carr, *What is History?* 21.

[210] F. Cantor and Richard I Schneider, *How to Study History*, 256.

a commitment to truth based on rationality. However, rationality became rationalization!!"[211] After modernism comes post-modernity and this does not entertain modernism's dedication to truth based on scientific surveillance. Consequently, for the post-modernists, the concept of "absolute" does not prevail which leads to the actuality that there can be no ultimate truth. Every story is an invented story. Fact is a delusion or a fantasy which evolves out of conventional behaviours.[212]

To put it briefly, facts and documents about the past are indispensable to historical restoration. Yet, the important issue of the historian's relation with his/her facts divides contemporary historians. One stand asserts that not all the past is recoverable and that the legality of the facts rests on the *priori* (presumptive) choice of the historian. The commonly accepted terms that "facts speak for themselves" are modified by the maxim that "facts speak only when the historian calls on them: it is he [sic] who decides to which facts to give the floor and in what order or context."[213] Every historian has his/her own judgment to make. If a historian fails to build up his/her own inferences and judgments, he/she cannot circumspectly work as "no witness simply hands down a complete, photograph-like description of an event; rather he [sic] selects, alters, interprets and rationalizes."[214] Historical facts hence rely profoundly upon the historian's choice, selection, and interpretation of the facts by his/her intellectual as well as emotional processes. Therefore, a historian without the facts of history is rootless and pointless whereas the facts in the absence of their historian are futile and insignificant.[215] Suffice here to reiterate that there is nothing called the facts and that a historian creates facts to establish his/her understanding of the past.

---

[211] V. V. Thomas, *Dalit and Tribal Christians*, 34.

[212] For detailed elaboration see V. V. Thomas, *Dalit and Tribal Christians*, 34, 35.

[213] Carr, *What is History?* 11.

[214] Van A. Harvey, *The Historian and the Believer* (Bloomsbury Street, London: SCM Press Ltd, 1967), 41.

[215] See Carr, *What is History?* 30.

This being the case in history writing, all writers of Indian Christianity indisputably have their biases. Consequent to this, various styles of presenting historical facts are produced which may be explored as follows:

10.3. Early Indian Christian Historiography

10.3.1. Colonial and Missionary Historiography

Even though Indian Christianity is much older than Western Christianity, Christianity in India is viewed by followers of other living faiths as the White people's religion because Indian Christian historiography had been dominated by Western Christian historiography which had been written in the context of the role of the West about the rest of the world. Since the Europeans shaped the early Indian Christian historiography, their perspective was highlighted by neglecting the Indian perspective.[216] Early colonial and missionary history writing may be studied as follows.

One of the earliest books, as regards the history of Christianity in India, was written by Mathurin Veysierre de la Croze, a French Protestant in the employ of the King of Prussia who wrote a general history of India and has it published in 1724. The book intentionally left out many crucial Catholic histories in India. He focused on the Christians of Malabar and the Roman Catholic attempts to bring them under the Roman Catholic fold. His main motive was to bring to light the first Protestant mission to India which began in 1706.[217]

That was followed by James Hough's multi-volume work in 1839, 1845 and, posthumously, in 1860. He was a Minister of Ham, Surrey and later joined the East India Company on the Madras Establishment as a Chaplain.[218] He was interested in preaching the

---

[216] Potana Venkateswara Rao, "Christian Historiography: Changing Perspectives and Approaches in the Study of Christianity in India," in *Global Journal for Research Analysis,* 3/7 (July, 2014): 146-147.

[217] Cf. John C. B. Webster, *Historiography of Christianity in India,* 2nd ed. (New Delhi: Oxford University Press, 2014), 15. Hereafter cited as John C. B. Webster, *Historiography.*

[218] See James Hough, *Informations and Suggestions for the Use of Missionaries, Missionary Candidates and Committees* (London: Hatchard and Son, 1832), i.

Gospel to people of other faiths and was even enthusiastic about building up the Indian Church. He took up the work of writing and began justifying Protestant missions against the Roman Catholic Church.

The first two volumes of Hough's books dealt especially with the Syrian Christians and Roman Catholics up to 1750 in which the Synod of Diamper occupies a prominent position. The latter three volumes concentrate on Protestant Christian history. Hough's motive seems to describe the failure of the Syrian Christians and Roman Catholic Mission while bringing to light the triumph of the Protestant Mission. A. M. Mundadan is right when he evaluates Hough's works in the following words: "The author's main interest was to show that the Roman Catholic Mission was a story of failure and the Protestant Mission was one of success."[219] Apart from his history books, he wrote several letters to the editors of various periodicals defending Protestant missions in India,[220] most of which dealt with his criticisms of Roman Catholic missions. This is one example of "selective history writing."

Another historian was Abbe J. A. Dubois, a priest of the Parish Missionary Society, who tried to justify the Roman Catholic mission, writing that it was not possible to make real converts to Christianity among the natives in India.[221] He even published *Hindu Manners, Customs and Ceremonies* in 1906.[222] His arguments that it was difficult to convert Indians were based on three presumptions. First, there is native prejudice against Christianity. Second, Christian converts came from a Hindu background which is based on stern casteism. Consequently, Christian converts do not have an inner conversion. They clung to old superstitions and usages. Third, the new Bible translation was not reliable and even the Catholic Church

---

[219] O. L. Snaitang, "From Church History to History of Christianity - Historiographical Issues in the Study of Missiology in India," *Mission and Evangelism,* edited by Somen Das (Delhi: ISPCK, 1998), 136.

[220] See John C. B. Webster, *Historiography,* 16.

[221] See John C. B. Webster, *Historiography,* 17.

[222] See Abbe J. A. Dubois and Henry K. Beauchamnp, *Hindu Manners, Customs and Ceremonies* (London: Clarendon Press, 1906).

which seemed to be more appealing to Indians did not fare well in its enterprises.[223]

William Ward's book, *A View of the History, Literature and Religion of the Hindoos* (1817-1820) also believed that Indians were full of immorality, corruption, and cruelty and that the British were the only nation that was fit enough to tame the disruptive and unruly Indians.[224] This is an example of a "biased history."

One of the earliest essential histories of Indian Christianity was not written by the Orientalists but by their immense adversaries, the officials of the East India Company as well as the missionaries who tried to find out vulnerable points in the Hindu religion to win converts and consolidate the British Empire in India. The Oriental despotism on the part of the administrators and the missionaries gave way for the British to present the British government in India as the medium for changing the alleged corrupted Indian society. That was to the British the *raison d'être,* assignment of the British rule of India.[225]

On the one hand, this particular historiography seems to serve no useful purpose for Indian people. What is distressing here is that the Indian Christian history at this time was written not for the sake of Indian people and Indian Christians but for the sake of Western readers. On the other hand, it is not full of futile elements in the sense that they gave us "sources" which are like precious pearls on sea shores, whose place can never be washed away by any tide. Stating this, whether the sources Western writers gave us are authentic or not is a thing to really mull over. They gave us sources that they deemed important for them and their enterprises. They missed

---

[223] For detailed elaboration see Vanlalchhuanawma, "History leh Ziak Dan Thar Lo Chhuah Dan," (History and the Development of New Style of Writing) *Didakhe* 56/2 (March-April, 2017): 6. Hereafter cited as Vanlalchhuanawma, "History leh Ziak Dan Thar."

[224] Shashi Bhushan Upadhyay, *Historiography in the Modern World – Western and Indian Perspectives* (New Delhi: Oxford University Press, 2016), 426. Hereafter cited as Upadhyay, *Historiography in the Modern World.*

[225] Cf. E. Sreedharan, *A Textbook of Historiography - 500 BC to AD 2000,* reprint (New Delhi: Orient Blackswan, 2014), 423. Hereafter cited as Sreedharan, *A Textbook of Historiography.*

out on important sources which may give important information to the general Indian masses as generalizations made by colonialist historians were grossly exaggerated.

The direction of historiography we find at this stage is that early Indian Christian histories aimed initially at the outright denunciation and blame of the Indian life and culture, conversion of Indians from Hinduism to Christianity as their conversion, according to the colonial version, was not genuine, to the edificatory nature of British rule that taught and educated Indians from their state of utter darkness.[226] This tendency could have been caused by the Evangelical's pressure on the British colonial government to consider that the imperial purpose should be to enlighten the Indians who live in darkness, even though early British colonizers were not sympathetic to that suggestion,[227] and sometimes were rather discourteous towards the preaching of the Gospel.

10.3.2. Protestant Historiography

Protestant historiography is about a particular denomination or institution written from the insider's perceptions which are generally called ecclesiastical imperialism which can be both biased and dominant in its perspective. This is what is christened "institutional historiography" or "ecclesiastical historiography."[228] This historiography takes importance to the Church, its initiatives, expansion, and development which was resolutely directed towards the Protestant fold only. It was as exclusive as possible and, ironically, imperialistic too!

In 1875 Rev. M. A. Sherring published *The History of Protestant Missions in India, from their Commencements in 1706 to 1871.* The book serves to fuel the zeal of the Churches at home in support of the huge venture of Missions in India.[229] Sherring dealt with the escalation of the Protestant Church across India by giving a region-wise portrayal of Christianity in India. He commended Protestant

---

[226] Cf. Sreedharan, *A Textbook of Historiography*, 423.

[227] See Upadhyay, *Historiography in the Modern World*, 425.

[228] Vanlalchhuanawma, "History leh Ziak Dan Thar," 6, 7.

[229] See John C. B. Webster, *Historiography*, 26.

missionary works and gave credit to them for the awakening of India in its present form. For Sherring, "the history of Christianity in India was the triumphant story of missions, missionaries, and missionary methods."[230] This model of "glorified history" is more valued and dearer for the Westerners than the Indian Christians.

Sir John William Kaye's *Christianity in India: a Historical Narrative* (1859) dealt with the Church-state relationship. Kaye, like Sherring, spoke highly of Protestant missionary undertaking in India. He gave some space to put in the record the works of the British colonial administration for the upliftment of Indian society.[231] He urged the British government not to impose Christianity in government-run schools and supplemented that it is a good Christian principle that always triumphs over forceful imposition.

Another Protestant history book produced was Julius Richter's *A History of Missions in India,* published first in German in 1906 and later in English in 1908.[232] This book concentrates on the growth and development of missions in India.

The history books published during this time were written by Western authors and were published in the West for a Western readership. They were more precious in the West than in India. The histories were essentially designed to put in the written record the efforts of missionaries to establish the Christian Church in India and not the history of the Indian Christians and the Church in India *per se.*

The chief aim, therefore, was to "stimulate the zeal of the Churches at home on behalf of the great enterprise of missions in India."[233] Thus, in the Protestant historiography, the Indian Church and native Indians did not occupy the nucleus of history and, India and Indian Christianity became the vital platform for the missionaries to perform their religious acts upon. In their spacious

---

[230] John C. B. Webster, *Historiography,* 28.

[231] See John C. B. Webster, *Historiography,* 25, 26.

[232] See John C. B. Webster, *Historiography,* 31.

[233] M. A. Sherring, *The History of Protestant Missions in India, from their Commencements in 1706 to 1871* (London: Trubner and Co., 1875), viii.

historical stage, Western writers made use of mission sources to strengthen their stands which were used uncritically, without serious evaluation of sources. This was basically done to raise funds for the growth of the missionary works as well as to glorify their missionary undertakings.

10.3.3. Roman Catholic Historiography

Catholic historians differ from their Protestant counterparts in their styles of writing. They did not take account of the general history of Christianity in India equivalent to those of Hough, Kaye, or Richter. Rev. M. D'sa published two volumes of Catholic history which are *History of the Roman Catholic Church in India,* published in 1910 and 1924.[234] These volumes were one of the early history books which covered the Roman Catholic enterprises in India. Since the book's anticipated readers were Catholic members, he wittingly avoided controversies[235] which others would be inquisitive of.

Another book published was *A South Indian Mission: The Madura Catholic Mission from 1535 to 1935,* written by Joseph C. Houpert SJ.[236] What can be perceived from his book were the organizational continuity of the Roman Catholic Church and the missionary growth and development[237] of the Madura Mission or Madurai Mission in South India which was a Jesuit Missionary movement that had its starting point at Madura and extended thence over the Eastern half of the peninsula. Houpert supported missionary methods of the Roman Catholic Church in India like

---

[234] There are two volumes of M. D'Sa's books which are *History of the Catholic Church in India, Vol. I: A.D. 52-1652* (Bombay: The Lalka Printing and Litho Works, 1910) and *History of the Catholic Church in India, Vol.II: A.D. 1652-1924* (Bombay: The Lalka Printing and Litho Works, 1924). The first volume is about the establishment and spread of Christianity in India whereas the second one gives the accounts of Papal and Portuguese documents pertaining to the jurisdiction of the *Padroado* in India.

[235] See John C. B. Webster, *Historiography,* 36.

[236] Joseph C. Houpert SJ, *A South Indian Mission: the Madura Catholic Mission from 1535 to 1935,* new ed. (Trichinopoly: St. Joseph's Industrial School Press, 1937).

[237] See John C. B. Webster, *Historiography,* 36, 37.

Robert de Nobili, Antony de Vico, and the subsequent priests of the Madura Mission.

To wrap up in short, Western writers presented Indian history with European readership in mind. Their history books were published in the West. These histories belonged to the West rather than to India. Therefore, the history of Christianity was observed as the history of missions and missionaries from the West, their failures, and successes. This holds for the historiography of Christianity in India both in the nineteenth and early twentieth centuries. Therefore, the history in these periods can be labelled as a "mission history" or "missionary perspective of Indian history." It can scarcely be called history. What is striking here is that all the histories during this specific time have nothing serious to do with Indian Christianity at all and that Indian Christians were projected as mere objects of missionary debates.

As mentioned earlier, the perspective espoused by Protestant historiography posits that foreigners orchestrated a theatrical performance on Indian soil, thereby advancing an imperialistic worldview. Conversely, Catholic historical accounts adopt a more nuanced approach to interpreting the same events, with less emphasis placed on imperialistic ideals.[238] The choice of historical narrative can have a profound impact on our understanding of the past. By adopting a more critical and refined approach, we can gain a deeper understanding of the complexities and contradictions of historical events, and move toward a more accurate and comprehensive understanding of our shared history.

10.3.4. Colonial and Missionary Alliance and the Historiography thereof

Even though colonial rulers and missionaries disagreed on different premises during their heyday in India, it is crystal clear that the two had an analogous attempt that is consolidation and extension of the British colony in India. While colonial administrators broke the breakup of the world into two camps – the European and the Oriental, the traditional Christian Evangelicals made a distinction

[238] John C. B. Webster, *Historiography*, 37.

not between the European and the Oriental but between the lost and the saved. Colonizers concentrated on the strengthening of the British Empire which concerned the earthly kingdom. Missionaries, on the other hand, disparaged and sneered at the social and cultural traits of India simply because of their need for financial and moral support from the people from whom they came. They projected themselves as the solitary knight in shining armour to save the Indians from their unfathomable physical and spiritual bondage. Indeed, Indian religions, according to their versions were crammed with evil elements while they did not have a grasp of what Indian religions really were. Missionaries failed to look at their contemporary Indian society from an indigenous point of view and thus developed a superior view which led the former to see only the dark side of the latter. Colonizers and evangelists could not be separated albeit inconsistencies arose in between.[239] De Gruchy justly commented:[240]

> The construction and extension of God's reign somehow found its analogy, and more, in the construction and extension of Victoria's reign; their (missionaries') prayer for universal peace was linked to Pax Britannica; and their vision of the coming kingdom was undoubtedly linked in some way with the birth of a new century. Victoria was not only an example of a righteous ruler but also an example to all foreign chiefs of one whose reign was blessed because she believed in Christ...they gladly aligned their missionary cause with the extension of her benign and righteous rule.

[239] See V. V. Thomas, "A Survey of the Recent Historiographical Developments in India Including that of the Dalit and Tribal Movements," in *Methodological Issues in Theological Research – An Exploration,* edited by H. Vanlalauva (Serampore: Department of Research/SATHRI, 2014), 169, 170. Hereafter cited as V. V. Thomas, "A Survey."

[240] John W. De Gruchy, "Who Did They Think They Were – Some Reflections from a Theologian on Grand Narratives and Identity in the History of Missions," in *The Imperial Horizons of British Protestant Missions, 1880-1914,* edited by Andrew Porter (Grand Rapids, Michigan: William B. Eerdmans Publishing Company, 2003), 216.

It is, therefore, crystal clear that their rule was never criticized nor challenged!

Even with the existence of disparities in their historiographical approaches, the harmony of colonial and missionary historiography can be brought to light which may be studied as follows. Almost all the historians were Western authors who presented Indian Christianity as an extension of Western Christianity. Stories of missionaries are told in such a way that they were conquerors, leading actors, warriors, and heroes. Colonial and missionary histories were dominated by male-oriented history. Moreover, native contributions have been either silenced or sidelined. Lastly, local rituals, practices, and customs have not been given due respect.[241]

10.4. Revolutionizing Shifts, Transitions and Trajectories

10.4.1. Nationalist Historiography

The colonial and Christian interpretation of India presented India in a downbeat and pessimistic way. Those imperialist and missionary challenges to Indian society had to be met and the Hindu religion and its revered books, the first object of Christian attack, needed to be protected and defended.[242] In this background, Indian reformers such as Rammohun Roy, Dayanand Saraswati, and Vivekananda stood up and tried to breathe new life into Indian religion and society or older Hinduism through reform movements that are sometimes referred to as a "Protestanisation of Hinduism." This was also the beginning of the Indian Renaissance. It was the fear of Christianity that created a "wake-up" in Hinduism. "By equating India's ancient past with a Hindu past, it framed the argument for an exclusivist and homogenous definition of ancient Indian society, presuming as well the existence of a well-defined religion called Hinduism for the

---

[241] For detailed elaboration on harmony of colonial and missionary elaboration see V. V. Thomas, "A Survey," 170.

[242] Cf. Sreedharan, *A Textbook of Historiography*, 429.

ancient period."[243] This is obviously a transition from that of the colonial historiography to that of a nationalist one.

The view of the reformers led to a growing appetite for history among the Indian scholars. Consequently, the educationist Ishwar Chandra Bidyasagar wrote *Bangala Itihas* (History of Bengal) in 1848 and Kedar Nath Datta *Bharatbarsher Itihas* (History of India) in 1859. The Indian writers in this era tended to depict the Indian ancient age as a golden era and concluded that the following era of Muslim rule was one of failure and loss. More and more history were used to challenge many of the long-suffering suppositions of the Orientalists. Thus, Partha Chatterjee firmly believes that by 1870 the primary constituents of a nationalist historiography were already in place. The first home-grown writings about an Indian past were seen in the 1850s which affirmed that the depiction of the past could be done more accurately in Bengali rather than English. What can be ascertained here is that language was now starting to be identified as a key and a manifestation of identity[244] which provided for the rising national consciousness.

Colonial Western education was thus confronted and challenged by Bengali education. This union of colonial education with the vernacular led to the new historiography. The new school textbooks tried to revitalize pride in the Indian legacy and custom by arguing the derision of the colonial accounts. Kshirodchandra Raychaudhuri wrote in the preface of his book in 1876, "I have written this book for those who have been misled by translations of histories written in English,"[245] which enlightens us that educated Indians were fed up with Western historiography.

In another word, we can say that a new approach to Indian history writing appeared on the scene to resist imperialist historiography, which is dearly called "nationalist historiography."

---

[243] Georg G. Iggers and Edward Wang, *A Global History of Modern Historiography* (Noida: Dorling Kindersley, 2010), 102. Hereafter cited as Georg G. Iggers and Edward Wang, *A Global History.*

[244] See Georg G. Iggers and Edward Wang, *A Global History*, 106.

[245] See Ranajit Guha, *An Indian Historiography of India: A Nineteenth Century Agenda and Its Implications* (Calcutta: Centre for Studies in Social Science, 1988), 42.

This developed in the late nineteenth century. The tendency and the character of the British writers provoked Indian thinkers to respond to defend their country. The sarcastic comment of English historian Edward Thompson made this clear, which goes, "Indians are not historians, and they rarely show any critical ability...So they are not likely to displace our account of our connection with India."[246] This was the common understanding among the Westerners.

The question of whether Nationalist historians represented Indians as a whole or only the elite class deserves our serious attention. Ranajit Guha, a subaltern historian, convincingly states that the formation of India as a nation and the growth of nationalistic awareness were totally elite achievements and that these successes are credited to Indian elite personalities, institutions, activities, and ideas.[247] According to him, "Elitist historiography of the nationalist or neo-nationalist type is primarily an Indian practice."[248] What is left out of this historiography is the "politics of the people", the failure of which may be attributed to the inadequacy of the bourgeoisie.[249] This makes it clear that the Nationalist historiography does not represent the people of India as a whole.

One of the earliest histories written from a nationalist perspective is Romesh Chunder Dutt's, *A History of Civilization in Ancient India,*[250] published in three volumes from 1889 to 1891. He stressed the infinite spiritual superiority of Hinduism and in doing so also attempted to show that ancient India was almost up to Modern Europe in scientific achievements. According to him, "the history of the intellectual and religious life of the ancient Hindu is matchless in

---

[246] Edward Thompson, *The Other Side of the Medal* (London: Hogarth Press, 1925), 27-28.

[247] Ranajit Guha, "On Some Aspects of the Historiography," in *Subaltern Studies I: Writings on South Asian History and Society,* edited by Ranajit Guha (New Delhi: Oxford University Press, 1982), 1. Hereafter cited as Ranajit Guha, "On Some Aspects of the Historiography."

[248] Ranajit Guha, "On Some Aspects of the Historiography," 1.

[249] Ranajit Guha, "On Some Aspects of the Historiography," 6, 7.

[250] Romesh Chunder Dutt, *A History of Civilization in Ancient India* (Calcutta: Thacker, Spink & Co., 1891).

its continuity, its fullness and, its philosophical truth."[251] His other book, *The Economic History of India* (1902 and 1904) is exemplary in critiquing the imperial British policy in India. He also translated the *Rig Veda* in Bengali (1885 to 1887), *Mahabharata* (1899) *and Ramayana* (1900)[252] into English.

V. K. Rajwade spent his entire life in the collection and publication of source materials which would prove useful for writing nationalist histories. He resisted financial help from institutions and the colonial government as he believed that help would jeopardize his exploration of truth. He published thousands of documents as the Sources of Maratha History in twenty-two volumes 1898 and 1922[253] which received sincere acclamation.

Kaj Baago, T. V. Philip, D. V. Singh, George Thomas and the like objected to the Euro-centric approach to the spreading, growth, and augmentation of Christianity in India. They concentrated their writings on demonstrating how Indian Christianity has been in a continuation and how genuinely Indian identity for Christianity has been enlarging because of the relations between social and religious aspects. "Indianization and indigenization were some of the major themes of their narration."[254]

Bankim Chandra Chatterji, Chandra Nath Basu, Raj Narain Bose and the like acted in response to the attack of the missionaries and stood in defence that Indian philosophy outshined others even in ancient times. Swami Dayanand Saraswati, Swami Vivekananda, and others recollected the past glory of India. R. C. Datta's *Civilization in Ancient India* was meant to answer questions,

---

[251] R. C. Dutt, *Early Hindu Civilization*, 4th ed. (Calcutta: Punthipustak, 1963), 3. Originally published in 1888.

[252] See Sunil Sen, "Romesh Chandra Dutt," *Historians and Historiography in Modern India,* edited by S. P. Sen (Calcutta: Institute of Historical Studies, 1973), 320.

[253] See Upadhyay, *Historiography in the Modern World,* 463.

[254] Vanlalchhuanawma, "Methodological Issues in the Study of History of Christianity," in *Methodological Issues in Theological Research – An Exploration,* edited by H. Vanlalauva (Serampore: Department of Research/SATHRI, 2013), 211. Hereafter cited as Vanlalchhuanawma, "Methodological Issues in the Study of History of Christianity."

especially about the caste system in India's past. Mookerji's *Fundamental Unity of India* attempted to show that India had unity in diversity[255] as its principle in ancient days.

10.4.2. Indian Nationalism from the Subaltern Perspective

Subaltern thinkers consider that the contributions, involvements, and participation of the people in the lower strata of society are not satisfactorily recognized in the written record of the nationalist movement. It is to be kept in mind that modern Christian subaltern historians also argue in the same vein. Therefore, a contemporary prominent historian for the cause of the subalterns V. V. Thomas rightly says, "The way the history of the conversion movement is written seems to say that the people were mere recipients of the Gospel without having any discernment."[256] This needs serious consideration.

Ranajit Guha, the pioneer of Subaltern Historiography, is also correct when he states that, "The historiography of Indian nationalism for a long time has been dominated by elitism – colonialist elitism and bourgeois-nationalist elitism."[257] In this historiography, according to him, the subalterns are not given an equitable place despite their sufferings and loss for the sake of Indian nationalism. What is stressed here is the prominence of leaders like Mahatma Gandhi and the like. This historiography lifts these prominent figures to laudable status. Furthermore, the lowly and the voiceless are always projected as having no thinking of their own. Even if they have their framework of mind, that is classified as lower than that of the leaders. In this milieu, there is no denying that the subalterns act for the elite.[258]

Nationalist history has been dominated by accounts of privileged and selected elites whose stories most of the time being told by the elites themselves. That is one of the main factors which

---

[255] K. L. Khurana, *Concepts and Methods of Historiography,* 8th ed. (Agra: Lakhsmi Narayan Agarwal, 2017), 380.

[256] V. V. Thomas, *Dalit and Tribal Christians*, 48.

[257] Ranajit Guha, "On Some Aspects of the Historiography," 1.

[258] See V. V. Thomas, *Dalit and Tribal Christians*, 49.

cause contemporary subaltern historians to re-write history which gives justice to the unprivileged masses.[259] This task carries not only the inclusion of the subalterns in historical accounts but also recognises and brings to broad daylight their role as agencies and subjects in the making of a society and the nation at large.

Nationalist historiography has its merits and demerits. There has been a growing tendency which stress that marginalized masses and their part in the making of the nation, in the struggle for independence and every aspect of life is not satisfactorily represented by early historians. Ranajit Guha, M. S. S. Pandian, Gayatri Chakravorty Spivak, Gyan Prakash and others are renowned in this field. From their writings, it can be discerned that ordinary people do not figure in the nationalist history. This led to the beginning of writing history from post-patriarchal, subaltern, Dalit, tribal, and feminist standpoints.[260]

In its softer corner, Indian nationalism has a methodological slip. To take one example, a nationalist historian, K. P. Jayaswal, author of *Hindu Polity* (1924) purposely added interpretations on words and passages in inscriptions and literary texts. A. L. Basham tells of how K. P. Jayaswal wrote his history in the following way:[261]

> To prove his thesis Jayaswal employed a large range of sources, but used them in the manner of a barrister trying to win a favourable judgment, emphasizing every passage which tended to support his case, and interpreting it in the most favourable light, while virtually ignoring the evidence which went against him.

Jayaswal gave too much weight to the role of the native ruling dynasties in liberating India from Shakas and Kushans. He is also

---

[259] See V. V. Thomas, *Dalit and Tribal Christians*, 50.

[260] See V. V. Thomas, *Dalit and Tribal Christians*, 48-50.

[261] A. L. Basham, "Modern Historians of Ancient India," in *Historians of India, Pakistan and Ceylon,* edited by C. H. Philips (London: Oxford University Press, 1977), 283.

criticized for projecting modern nationalist ideas into ancient institutions.[262]

Furthermore, Sreedharan deems that Nationalist Historiography over-emphasizes the Indian past. He considers it true that the Indian origin of the Aryans, the pre-Harappan antiquity of the Vedic culture, the denial of foreign influence on Indian civilization and the existence of political unity from the earliest times were all part of the glorification of India's past.[263] "The deep conviction in India's past glory sometimes led historians to stretch their arguments to an obnoxious and ridiculous extent... we are informed that there were firearms and aeroplanes in the age of the Epics."[264]

On the other hand, Indian nationalist historiography has its strength and vigour in the sense that it served as a stimulant of historical studies in India. An offshoot of Indian nationalism is a growth of interest in historical studies. The nationalist spirit gave flame to the work of historical research.[265] Another important dynamism of Indian nationalism is that it incited growth of interest in regional and local history. It inspires us to study more of regional and local culture, customs and values which voluntarily or involuntarily increase archaeological works in hitherto unexplored areas. This, in turn, fills the lacunae of history or historical writing. Thus, Indian nationalist historiography enhances the in-depth and meticulous study of a confined history of both the plains people and the hills people alike and serves as a testimony that "evidence of historical variations in the cultural pattern led to the recognition that it was unwise and unhistorical to generalize about the entire Indian subcontinent based on the history of the Ganges heartland."[266]

To reiterate, European scholars tried to elevate the British government while justifying every bit of the British government's

---

[262] See R. S. Sharma, *Rethinking India's Past* (New Delhi: Oxford University Press, 2009), 273.

[263] For detailed elaboration see Sreedharan, *A Textbook of Historiography*, 434.

[264] Sreedharan, *A Textbook of Historiography*, 434.

[265] See Sreedharan, *A Textbook of Historiography*, 435.

[266] Sreedharan, *A Textbook of Historiography*, 436.

efforts to rule India. Their history highlighted and applauded only the bright side of the British government and continuously repeated that Indian civilization was full of trouble that necessitated the sending of missionaries to India. In the beginning, Indian scholars responded defensively but as time went on, they concentrated on studying India's past splendour and glory which inspired patriotic feelings among the Indian masses.

10.4.3. Shifts and Transitions by way of CHAI Historiography

A completely new trajectory appeared in the historiography of Christianity in India with the introduction of the Church History Association of India (CHAI) Historiography. The CHAI was founded in 1935[267] and came forward to start writing the history of Christianity from an Indian perspective, as against Western writing. Western missionaries bore the torch of the Gospel across the globe with Western culture as a dominating force. They disfigured and misrepresented the true Gospel idea as well as the history of Christianity in native places intentionally or unintentionally. "This has also been reflected in the development of Christian history in India,"[268] which projects Christianity in India as dependent on Western mother Churches for their birth, growth, and nourishment. Furthermore, the Indian Church has been presented as an isolated phenomenon of a special little world. This is what is called the Western perspective. The Indian perspective differs from this in the sense that Indians know that Christianity was in India before the arrival of Western missionaries,[269] and that the Indian Church has been closely linked with the secular history of the country.[270]

The CHAI historiography came as a challenge to the Western notion that Indian Christian endeavour was an eastward addition

[267] See Merithung Tungoe, *Administrators Missionaries and a World Turned Upside Down* (Delhi: ISPCK, 2000), 21. Hereafter cited as Merithung Tungoe, *Administrators.*

[268] V. V. Thomas, *Dalit and Tribal Christians*, 55, 56.

[269] See V. V. Thomas, *Dalit and Tribal Christians*, 52.

[270] Frederick S. Downs, "Editorial," in *Indian Church History Review* 13/2, 1979, 1.

of Western ecclesiastical history.[271] The project visualized that such a history ought to be written in the context of the social, religious, political and cultural history of the people of India rather than an additional room of Christianity from the West.

The core rationale of CHAI is to encourage investigation in Indian Church history, chiefly with a vision of producing a standard work for the history of Christianity in India. That must be done with a watchful study and research of all the facts, records and manuscripts available for the research.[272] Consequently, a six-volume of History of Christianity in India had to be written and published including all the regions throughout the country. In its directive, it insists that the history "should be written from a single perspective, should be directed primarily towards an academic and Indian readership…"[273] As of now, five volumes[274] had already been published.

The CHAI adopted four important tools or approaches for writing Indian Christian history such as socio-historical, regional, national, and ecumenical approaches. The CHAI's regional approach distinguishes CHAI history from traditional histories of missions in India, the latter of which are dominated by denominational aspects, not by regions.[275] The National Approach is to give importance to the nationalistic experience of the Indian Christian communities. Indian Christians desired

---

[271] See V. V. Thomas, *Dalit and Tribal Christians.*

[272] See Editorial, *Indian Church History Review* I/1 (June, 1967): 1

[273] A. M. Mundadan, *History of Christianity in India, Vol I: From the Beginning up to the Middle of the Sixteenth Century,* (Bangalore: CHAI, 1989), vii.

[274] The books published so far are as listed as follows: Volume I - A. M. Mundadan, *History of Christianity in India: From the Beginning up to the Middle of the Sixteenth Century*; Volume II – Joseph Thekkedath, *History of Christianity in India: From the Middle of the Sixteenth Century to the End of the Seventeenth* Century; Volume III- E. R. Hambye, *History of Christianity in India: Eighteenth* Century; Volume IV, Part 2 - Hugald Grafe, *History of Christianity in India: Tamil Nadu in the Nineteenth and Twentieth Centuries*; Volume V, Part 5 - Frederick S. Downs, *History of Christianity in India: North East India in the Nineteenth and Twentieth Centuries,*

[275] For detailed elaboration see A. Hmingthanzuala, "Historiographical Tools of Church History Association of India: Problems and Prospects for the Twenty First Century History of Christianity in India" (D.Th assessment paper, SATHRI, 2017). Hereafter cited as A-a, "Historiographical Tools."

to project themselves as part of the Indian nation which became more sensible after India gained independence. As such, the CHAI perspective has a political overtone and it also seems noteworthy to announce visibly that Christianity had always been Indian,[276] even a fundamental part of the Indian nation.

Yet, the volumes of CHAI history published so far are not free from criticism as they failed to cover the national perspective as emphasized in the Scheme.[277] The first volume written by Mundadan almost completely concentrates on the history of the St. Thomas Christians in Kerala and their encounters with the Portuguese.[278] The two volumes were written by Thekkedath[279] and Hambye[280] cover as wide an area as possible but depict the history of Christianity region-wise. What can be perceived as national peace is found only in a few words in the introduction and conclusion parts.[281] The remaining three volumes on the North East, Tamil Nadu, and North West gave a spotlight on the respective regions.[282]

---

[276] See A-a, "Historiographical Tools," 32.

[277] The "Scheme" came about as a resolution taken by CHAI in its triennial meeting at Dharmaram College, Bangalore in 1973 constituting an Editorial Board. The Editorial Board met the next year in 1974 and formulated the resolution in the form of a "Scheme" which provides Indian researchers with a guiding principle relevant to Indian context. See Vanlalchhuanawma, "Methodological Issues in the Study of History of Christianity," 208, 209.

[278] See A. M. Mundadan, *History of Christianity in India: from the Beginning up to the Middle of the Sixteenth Century*, Volume I, 9-347; 476-521.

[279] Joseph Thekkedath, *History of Christianity in India: From the Middle of the Sixteenth Century to the End of the Seventeenth Century (1542 – 1700)*, Volume II (Bangalore: Church History Association of India, 2001).

[280] E. R. Hambye, *History of Christianity in India: Eighteenth Century*, Volume III (Bangalore: The Church History Association of India, 1997).

[281] Thekkedath, *History of Christianity in India: From the Middle of the Sixteenth Century to the End of the Seventeenth Century (1542 – 1700)*, Volume II, 1-9.

[282] Cf. F. S. Downs, *History of Christianity in India: North East India in the Nineteenth and Twentieth Centuries*; Grafe, *History of Christianity in India: Tamil Nadu in the Nineteenth and Twentieth Centuries*, and John C. B. Webster, *History of Christianity in India: North West India in the Nineteenth and Twentieth Centuries.*

Felix Wilfred thinks that even though the CHAI takes pride in publishing history books which have a different course and orientation from the previous ones, the books published so far have connections with mainline historical writings.[283] Walotemjen also feels that the religious dimension and its function in the conversion movement among the tribals is not given due credit in the CHAI books published so far[284] which needs to be seriously taken care of.

Even though the CHAI followed a new and vibrant course on the highway of Indian Christian historiography, the position of women in the CHAI history guidelines is acutely open to discussion. To take one issue for instance, members of the Editorial Board consisted of male members only and the Board was not aware of the significance of the study of the position, role, and part played by women.[285] Moreover, when a resolution was made to publish a wide-ranging chronicle of Christianity in India, the CHAI, according to Mundadan, failed to give justice to the Dalits who form an imperative section of the Indian Christian community.[286] In so far as the CHAI history is concerned, the Dalit's history stays behind the others and is still jumbled and fragmentary. Another lacuna of the CHAI project is that it is still part of the mainline historical writing. Though F.S. Down's book[287] proves to be an important source of information for the readers, it does not faithfully unearth native peoples' participation. This may primarily be because the author is not an Indian.[288] That is why the need for native writers in place of foreigners could be aired.

---

[283] For detailed elaboration see Felix Wilfred, "Historiography of Indian Christianity, Some Reflections," *Vidyjyoti* 73/10 (October, 2009): 17.

[284] Walotemjen. "Methodological Issues and Historiography of Christianity in India," in *Mapping the Context: An Interdisciplinary Exploration,* edited by Imsenperong, Menjiwopong Jamir and Walotemjen (np: The Authors, 2011), 221.

[285] See A-a, "Historiographical Tools," 32.

[286] See A. M. Mundadan, "Changing Approaches to Historiography," *Indian Church History Review* 35/1 (June, 2001): 53.

[287] Frederick S. Downs, *History of Christianity in India: North East India in the Nineteenth and Twentieth Centuries*, Volume V, Part 5 (Bangalore: The Church History Association of India, 2003).

[288] See A-a, "Historiographical Tools," 27.

Furthermore, there arise new, indigenous, and home-grown Churches in the Indian scenario which do not have attachment or bond with traditional, institutionalized Churches. They may be independent, evangelical, post-evangelical, charismatic or Pentecostal in nature. These emerging Churches may have faced a dearth of historical accounts, records, and documents. But their historical sources can be established in their narrations, stories, songs, oral testimonies and may be on the scattered literary sources.[289] The CHAI-history guidelines need to blend in this vital new phenomenon in its perspective.

10.4.4. Postcolonial Historiography

The commencement of the Postcolonial perspective is another important transition in the writing of history in India which refers to the development of a new historiography that emerged as a protest against the colonial historiography.[290] Even though Edward Said's ground-breaking *Orientalism* (1978) was believed to be the inauguration of the emergence of postcolonial thought in historical writings, one cannot deny the fact that Frantz Fanon had already published books dealing with postcoloniality[291] even before formal postcolonial theory developed.

Fanon joined the Algerian liberation movement against French colonialism and framed his resistance to the tyrannical impact of colonialism. He had his *Black Skin, White Masks* published in 1952 in which he assailed the racial label created by colonialism, which identifies black as lower, almost sub-human.[292] In his second book, The *Wretched of the Earth* published in 1961 he considered the 'hybridity' caused by colonialism as traumatic and shocking, unlike

---

[289] See Roger Hedlund, "Approaches to Indian Church History in the Light of New Christian Movements," *Indian Church History Review,* IIIIV/2 (December, 2000): 165.

[290] Cf. Woba James, *Major Issues in the History of Christianity in India: A Post Colonial Reading* (Jorhat: TDCC, 2013), 11.

[291] See Upadhyay, *Historiography in the Modern World,* 682.

[292] See Upadhyay, *Historiography in the Modern World,* 682.

Bhabha[293] who rejoices in it.[294] He believed that the only liberation of the colonized can be achieved through entire annihilation of the colonial system: "At the level of individuals, violence is a cleansing force. It frees the native from his [sic] inferiority complex and from his [sic] despair and inaction; it makes him [sic] fearless and restores…self-respect."[295]

This cut-off point of the colonial discourse analysis that advanced into postcolonial theory has been essentially inaugurated by the publication of Edward Said's *Orientalism* in 1978.[296] It was this book, through an intense and sweltering critique of Western cultural production that kicked off postcolonial studies. Said focused on the making of the imperial dialogues and conversations and investigated the manners in which they represented and constructed the colonized land and its people.[297]

The term "postcolonialism" came to gain more popularity in 1989 with the publication of *The Empire Writes Back: Theory and Practice in Post-colonial Literatures* by Bill Ashcroft, Gareth Griffiths, and Helen Tiffin.[298] The writers used "postcolonial" to cover "all the culture affected by the imperial process from the moment of colonization to the present day. This is because there is a continuity of preoccupations throughout the historical process initiated by European imperial aggression."[299]

In *The Post-colonial Studies Reader*, edited by Bill Ashcroft, Gareth Griffiths and Helen Tiffin, the editors converse about postcolonialism and offered the following definitions: (1) an

---

293 Homi K. Bhabha is considered to be one of the most important theorists of postcolonialism. He introduced the idea of hybridity to show that the identities of both the colonizer and the colonized are split in the process of the colonial encounter. See Upadhyay, *Historiography in the Modern World*, 693, 694.

294 See Upadhyay, *Historiography in the Modern World*, 683, 684.

295 Upadhyay, *Historiography in the Modern World*, 684.

296 See Vanlalchhuanawma, "Methodological Issues in the Study of History of Christianity," 217.

297 See Upadhyay, *Historiography in the Modern World*, 687.

298 Cf. Upadhyay, *Historiography in the Modern World*, 680.

299 Bill Ashcroft, Gareth Griffiths and Helen Tiffin, *The Empire Writes Back: Theory and Practice in Postcolonial Literatures* (New York: Routledge, 1989), 2.

amorphous set of discursive practices akin to postmodernism, and (2) a more specific and historically located set of cultural strategies,[300] which is not to be perceived as an era that started only after independence as it is more expressive of the entirety of practices, in all their multiplicity, which portray the societies of the postcolonial world from the initiation of colonization up to this day. It has to be kept in mind that colonial hangover lingers even after the colonizers left the colonies and continues to take new avatar in a neo-colonial manner.[301]

Post-war writings have the tendency to incline towards "commonwealth" and "third world," principally in the realm of minority studies. These were substituted evidently in the 1990s by the term postcolonial. Writers use both the hyphenated "post-colonial" and unhyphenated "postcolonial" purposefully. According to Norman J. Wilson, "post-colonial" substitutes "postwar" in defining historical periodization, following the exit of the British and French from Africa, India, the Caribbean and other regions while the unhyphenated form "postcolonial" denotes a way of framing information. For him, it depicts a perspective or academic attitude that directs methodology.[302] Upadhyay takes his stand in this line, too. For him, the term "post-colonial" simply implies a particular historical era signifying the end of the colonial regime while "postcolonial" implies rigorous and broad critique of a mixture of cultural forms[303] surfacing out of the long colonial encounter.

Postcolonialism disparages colonialists for their Euro-centrism since colonialists disregard the role colonies played in shaping modern European culture and civilization. Postcolonialism makes itself different from the previous anti-colonial thought contained in Marxism and nationalism. It disapproves of Marxism as the latter

---

300 Bill Ashcroft, Gareth Griffiths and Helen Tiffin, eds, *The Post-colonial Studies Reader* (London: Routledge, 1995), xv.

301 Cf. Norman J. Wilson, *History in Crisis – Recent Directions in Historiography*, 3rd ed. (USA: Pearson, 2014), 127-129. Hereafter cited as Norman J. Wilson, *History in Crisis.*

302 Cf. Norman J. Wilson, *History in Crisis*, 127.

303 See Upadhyay, *Historiography in the Modern World*, 679.

maintains that all forms of oppression should be counted under the category of class, which fails to see the oppressed groups.[304] Postcolonialism deems nationalism as "a reverse or displaced legitimation of colonialism."[305] It believes that nationalism is trapped inside the colonial discourses,[306] using by and large prevailing European conceptual devices.

On the one hand, colonialism can be said to have commenced in the sixteenth century. On the other hand, we can say that it is an ageless feature of human contact from ancient days. "On an intellectual level, this definition would involve understanding how corporate groups exploit other corporate groups throughout history."[307] It covers the whole period "during" and "after" colonizers ruled in their colonized countries.

On its advantageous side, Norman J. Wilson is of the opinion that postcolonialism "offers an awareness of otherness in a comparative model that greatly exceeds the Euro-centrism of most Western history. It offers a method for evaluating dialogues of similarity and difference without being trapped in the binary model of the oppressor and oppressed."[308] Postcolonialism enables European historians to weigh up other systems of framing knowledge which does not necessarily mean a close or an end of European history, but somewhat a knowledge of otherness outside of European countries.[309]

The writers of "The Empire Writes Back" aptly pay homage to postcolonial literature based on three distinct observations: its emphasis on the relationship between colonizer and colonized as the primary source of creative and psychological impetus in writing; its expression of a shared past among members of the group; and

---

[304] See Upadhyay, *Historiography in the Modern World*, 680.

[305] Gayatri Chakravorty Spivak, *A Critique of Postcolonial Reason: Toward a History of the Vanishing Present* (Cambridge, Massachussets: Harvard University Press, 1999), 62.

[306] Cf. Upadhyay, *Historiography in the Modern World*, 680.

[307] Norman J. Wilson, *History in Crisis*, 127.

[308] Norman J. Wilson, *History in Crisis*, 137.

[309] Cf. Norman J. Wilson, *History in Crisis*, 137.

its hopeful vision of a more liberated and positive future.[310] The authors acknowledge that postcolonial literature is fundamentally concerned with the relationship between the colonizer and colonized, and that this relationship has been a key source of inspiration for writers. This literature serves to provide a unique perspective on the world, one that is informed by the experiences of those who have been colonized. Additionally, postcolonial literature seeks to express the shared history and experiences of those who have been colonized, creating a sense of community and connection among writers and readers alike. Finally, postcolonial literature often presents a vision of a more positive and liberated future, one that provides readers with hope and inspiration. In conclusion, postcolonial literature is a powerful and significant genre that speaks to the experiences of millions of people around the world. Through its focus on the relationship between colonizer and colonized, its expression of a shared past, and its hopeful vision of the future, postcolonial literature provides readers with a unique and valuable perspective on the world.

To evaluate, one of the basic flaws of postcolonialism is the supposition that the term postcolonialism can be "unbalanced" concerning women. Anne McClintock rightly penned down that "the promise of postcolonialism has been a history of hopes postponed (for women)."[311] The reason for this assertion is that the national bourgeoisies and kleptocracies that put on the shoes of postcolonial development and industrial modernization have been tremendously male. It has been a pity that equal access to the privileges and resources has never been granted to men and women. Requirements and desires of postcolonial nations have been basically identified with male arguments and conflicts, male desires, ambitions, and male welfare. Moreover, the very symbol

---

[310] Anne McClintock, "The Angel of Progress: Pitfalls of the Term Postcolonialism," in *Colonial Discourse/Postcolonial Theory,* edited by Francis Barker, Peter Hulme and Margaret Iversen (New Delhi: Viva Books, 2012), 255. Hereafter cited as Anne McClintock, "The Angel of Progress."

[311] Anne McClintock, "The Angel of Progress," 260.

of national power rests on the preceding constructions of gender power. Anne McClintock fittingly argues:[312]

> The global militarization of masculinity and the feminization of poverty have thus ensured that women and men do not live 'post-coloniality' in the same way, or share the same singular 'post-colonial condition'. In most countries, IMF and World Bank policy favoured cash-cropping and capital surplus in the systematic interests of men and formed a predictable pattern where men were given the training, the international aid, the machinery, the loans and cash. In Africa, women farmers produce 65-80 percent of all agricultural produce, yet do not own the land they work, and are consistently bypassed by aid programmes and 'development' projects.

What is more, another essential flaw of postcolonialism is the philosophical theory that colonial values have broadly and necessarily shaped every characteristic and rank of the colonized nation. Colonization has left its deep impact only on countries where colonization has a basic relationship with the colonized subjects. It is important to acknowledge that colonialism has had a significant impact on India's complex and diverse society. However, it is crucial for historians to avoid limiting their analysis of Christianity solely within the framework of this colonial process. Instead, a more refined and multifaceted approach is required to gain a comprehensive understanding of the role of religion[313] in this pluralistic society.

10.4.4.1. Subaltern as Methodology

Before the development and advancement of subaltern historiography, a French historian in the person of Georges Lefebvre coined the term "history from below" back in the 1930s. However, it gained significance only in the 1960s through the writings of British Marxist historian such as E. P. Thompson and

---

[312] See Anne McClintock, "The Angel of Progress," 260.

[313] See Vanlalchhuanawma, "Methodological Issues in the Study of History of Christianity," 218.

proponents like Emmanuel Le Roy Ladurie, Eric Hobsbawm and the like. In their writings, the centre of attention has shifted from the political history of elite groups to the new social, political, economic, and cultural histories. In this new history writing, the ordinary women, workers, farmers, and other subaltern groups started to be investigated and incorporated,[314] which is a much-welcomed move.

The sprouting and embryonic forms of subaltern historiography were found in Ranajit Guha's *Elementary Aspects of Peasant Insurgency in Colonial India*[315] which was originally published in 1983. This was followed by a series of writings including the volumes of Subaltern Studies[316] edited by Ranajit Guha as well as the works of other writers[317] strongly connected with the project.

A famous proponent of Subaltern Theory, Gayatri Spivak considers that Indians pen down our history as people whose awareness and realization have been fashioned as colonial subjects.[318]

---

[314] See Meeta Deka, "Folklore and Northeast Indian History," http://file.scirp.org/Html/7872.html (1 Aug. 2018), 2. Hereafter cited as Deka, "Folklore and Northeast Indian History."

[315] Ranajit Guha, *Elementary Aspects of Peasant Insurgency in Colonial India* (Durham: Duke University Press, 1999).

[316] The Subaltern Studies is the title given to a series of volumes which was published under Ranajit Guha as the editor. Guha was the engineer of the project. He edited the first six volumes of the Subaltern Studies. The other five volumes are edited by other scholars who have connection with the project. Right from the beginning the Subaltern Studies took the position that the entire tradition of Indian historiography before it has had elitist bias. The historians associated with the Subaltern Studies declared that they would set the position right by writing the history from the point of view of the common people. See Ranajit Guha, "Subaltern Approach to Indian History," http://ddceutkal.ac.in/Syllabus/MA_history/Paper_07.pdf (1 Sep. 2018).

[317] David Arnold, "Subaltern Studies – Then and Now," in *New Subaltern Politics – Reconceptualizing Hegemony and Resistance in Contemporary India,* edited by Alf Gunvald Niolsen, Srila Roy (New Delhi: Oxford University Press, 2015), 261.

[318] See Veena Das, "Subaltern as Perspective," in *Subaltern Studies VI – Writings on South Indian History and Society,* edited by Ranajit Guha (New Delhi: Oxford University Press, 1992), 310.

In order to free history writers from this colonial hangover rooted in their thoughts a new way of writing needed to be framed. In this juncture, subaltern studies as methodology surfaced in the writing of history in India with a view to displacing and dislocating the prominent place of European historians. This trend found its place in Indian historiography not only to reject western categories but also to indicate the launch of a new and independent relation to them. The subaltern studies are said to exhibit, "perhaps for the first time since colonialization," that "Indians are showing sustained signs of reappropriating the capacity to represent themselves (within the discipline of history)."[319]

The main schema of the subaltern history is that it was the repressed group of people such as peasants, agriculturists, factory workers, Dalits, Tribal and Adivasis who engineered the socio-cultural, political, and religious processes in India and not the colonial agencies or Indian elites. This is especially true in the national freedom movement of India. According to subaltern historians, all minor and depressed classes have their own self-created, independent subjectivity and previous Indian historiography normally closed the eyes to this independent subjectivity and the rebel consciousness of the Indian people.[320] Thus, the subaltern comes in as the maker of his/her own fate in these historical conversations.

10.4.4.1.1. Methodological Issues Involved in Subaltern Perspective

For quite a long time, historical writings or theological discussions from the West are by and large considered "normative" or "regulating" theology while theologies or historical writings from non-occidental countries are regarded as "indigenous" or "contextual." This has the tendency to lead people to suppose that the latter is relevant only to a situation or context and is deficient

---

[319] Ronald Inden, "Orientalist Constructions of India," in *Modern Asian Studies* 20/3 (1986): 445. As cited by Dipesh Chakrabarty, *Provincializing Europe – Postcolonial Thought and Historical Difference* (New Delhi: Oxford University Press, 2001), 27.

[320] For detailed elaboration see Vanlalchhuanawma, "Methodological Issues in the Study of History of Christianity," 215.

in "universal" standing. Subaltern historians are now convinced that all histories are contextual and that demographic reallocation from Euro-America to Asia and Africa takes place, following the transfer of the centre of history and theology as well.[321] This shifted the centre of historical writing from Europe and America to Asia, Africa, and Oceanic countries (Oceania, Australasia, or the Pacific). The shift has been wonderfully described by Dyron B. Daughrity in the following words:[322] "No longer is Christianity primarily a 'Northern' or 'Western' faith. The majority of Christians today live in the global South," "the twentieth century was 'hardly a success story' (for Western Europe)," "African Christianity... represents the turning over of a new leaf in world Christianity," and, "In fact, global Southerners often see the West as a grand mission field, a spiritual wasteland in need of the Gospel." This budge or reallocation of the centre of Christianity from the West to the global South prepares the way for the formerly sidelined and dominated third world countries to genuinely raise their voices in a more confident and relevant method.

Furthermore, looking at the scenario of Indian Churches, the practices and beliefs of Christians who come from lesser-known Churches are neglected in Indian Church history. The history of Christianity is generally understood and written from the stance of what Roger E. Hedlund calls "the "Great Tradition." "Little Tradition" of Indian Christianity remains unnoticed and sidelined. By and large, the story of Western Christianity, taking its root and firmly embedded in Indian soil remains noticed while the narrative of Indian Christianity goes unobserved.[323] Even if a history of Christianity is written at all, the accounts of this Little Tradition,

---

[321] Cf. K. Thanzauva, "Methodological Issues – Subaltern Perspectives," in *Methodological Issues in Theological Research – an Exploration,* edited by H. Vanlalauva, (Serampore: SATHRI, 2014), 106.

[322] Dyron B. Daughrity, *The Changing World of Christianity – the Global History of a Borderless Religion* (New York, Peter Lang Publishing Incorporation, 2010), 13, 91, 213, 254.

[323] See Roger E. Hedlund, "Approaches to Indian Church History in Light of New Christian Movements," *Indian Church History Review* 34/2 (December 2000): 153, 154.

where majority members belong to Dalit, Tribal and Adivasis go undocumented and unrecognized.

10.4.4.1.2. Evaluation of Subaltern Historiography

Subaltern historians tend to be harsh on previously existing styles of writing history in India. Some even go to the extreme that they view the historiographical past as void and take up the challenge of re-writing history basing only on their own resources. Previously, subaltern writers were criticized on their claim of a free domain and independent agency of the subalterns. Soon after, criticism came on the postcolonial bearing of subaltern historians.[324]

Secondly, the implicit insistence on an autonomous domain of the subaltern and by making it resistant to elite penetration excludes the possibilities of education, propaganda, and agitation, thus making the unity of theory and practice an impossibility. Moreover, whether this autonomous action is positive or negative in its consequences is not of much concern to subalternists: "It is a matter of indifference if it leads to communal rioting or united anti-feudal actions."[325]

Besides these, B. B. Chaudhuri disagrees with the thought of an autonomous subaltern sphere. Although certain distinctive ingredients are present in subalternity, "distinctiveness might not necessarily have derived from their autonomy."[326] David Ludden also criticizes making the inflexible distinction between the elite and the subaltern, forgetting all other hierarchical structures since such notion "resembles a concrete slab separating upper and lower space in a two-storey building. This hard dichotomy alienated subalternity from social histories that include more than two storeys or which

---

[324] See Upadhyay, *Historiography in the Modern World*, 562.

[325] Javeed Alam, "Peasantry, Politics and Historiography: Critique of New Trend in Relation to Marxism," in *Reading Subaltern Studies: Critical Histories, Contested Meaning and the Globalization of South Asia,* edited by David Ludden (Delhi: Permanent Black, 2002), 47-48, 52.

[326] B. B. Chaudhuri, "Subaltern Autonomy and the National Movement," in *Reading Subaltern Studies: Critical Histories, Contested Meaning and the Globalization of South Asia,* edited by David Ludden (Delhi: Permanent Black, 2002), 120-132.

move among them."[327] Moreover, as "subaltern politics was confined theoretically to the lower storey, it could not threaten a political structure.[328] This alienated subalternity from political histories of popular movements and alienated subaltern groups from organized, transformative politics.

10.4.4.2. Feminist Historiography

Since the subaltern historiography does not delve deep into exposing the distinct feminist dimension in its facet, a new way of writing history emerged which called for the inclusion of women in a written record which would bring justice and equality to history writing. It is a re-reading of history from a female perspective and is not just the history of feminism. It tries to explore and illuminate the female viewpoint of history through the rediscovery of female writers, artists, philosophers, etc., to recover and demonstrate the significance of women's voice and choices. For Jill Matthew, it is "to challenge the practices of the historical discipline that has belittled and oppressed women, and to create practices that allow women an autonomy and space for self-definition."[329] Feminism does not derive its theoretical conceptual base from any single theoretical formulation and no single person can be acclaimed to have defined feminism for all of us.[330] New approaches are being used to attempt to integrate women into the mainstream of historical development rather than isolating woman as a separate category.[331] Feminist historiography is not exclusively apprehensive of issues of gender *per se*, but rather

[327] David Ludden, ed., *Reading Subaltern Studies: Critical Histories, Contested Meaning and the Globalization of South Asia* (Delhi: Permanent Black, 2002), 16. Hereafter cited as David Ludden, *Reading Subaltern Studies.*

[328] See David Ludden, *Reading Subaltern Studies,* 16.

[329] "What is Feminist Historiography in Detail?" https://brainly.in/question/4567790 (5 Oct. 2018).

[330] Kamla Bhasin and Nighat Said Khan, *Some Questions on Feminism and its Relevance in South Asia,* reprint (New Delhi: Kali for Women, 2000), 3.

[331] A. D. Gordon et al., "The problem of Women's History," in *Liberating Women's History: Theoretical and Critical Essays* edited by Bernice A. Carroll (Urbana: University of Illinois Press, 1976), 75-92.

with the reinterpretation of history in a more holistic, reasonable and balanced manner.

The 1960s and 70s opened the ground for discussions and analysis to follow Phyllis Trible's *Depatriarchalizing in Biblical Interpretation*[332] and God and the Rhetoric of Sexuality.[333] What stood out of her observations was that the Bible was not ingenuously rejected but, the patriarchy inherent in the Bible was criticized. This was a beginning as well as a turning point for feminist discourse.

The late 1980s saw the flourishing of new advances and approaches which take into account not only the names of women in history writing but also allowed for their presence in the historical acts. Social history proves to be a useful tool for rediscovering the existence of women.[334] The more recent development came with sensitivity towards gender theory, "new essentialism," which tries to construct sexuality and gender theories receive much acceptance among feminist historians.

In Indian Christian feminist historiography, the publication of Narola Imchen's book, *Remembering our Foremothers*[335] is a watershed especially in Northeast Indian scenario. In her book, she deals about women's movement in Europe like anti-slavery movement and the like wherein she incorporated women activists like Lydia Child, the Grimke Sisters and many more. She examines how the American Baptist women missionaries, who were undertaking evangelization in Northeast India, were persuaded by the contemporary American women's movement. She highlights how women's movement received political thrust from the movement for the abolition of slavery. The

---

[332] Phyllis Trible, "Depatriachalizing in Biblical Interpretation," *JAAR* 41 (1973): 30-48.

[333] Phyllis Trible, *God and the Rhetoric of Sexuality* (Philadelphia: Fortress Press, 1978).

[334] See Rosy Zoramthangi, "Development of Methodological Trends in OT Study" (D.Th assessment paper, SATHRI, 2017). Hereafter cited as Rosy Zoramthangi, "Development of Methodological Trends."

[335] Narola Imchen, *Remembering our Foremothers – the Influence of the American Women's Movement on American Baptist Women Missionaries in Northeast India* (Jorhat: Women Study Department, ETC, 2003). Hererafter cited as Narola Imchen, *Remembering our Foremothers.*

bias and the prejudice that women experienced during the abolition movement encouraged them to fight against their own enslavement by men.[336] This book serves not only to highlight the role women play in history but also to electrify the zeal of women to work for the cause of the society they live in.

Attention-grabbing in this book is the impact of women's movement in Northeast India in the field of women's right, literature, temperance, education, and women's organizations. She wittingly writes how missionaries' wives were not treated as missionaries even though they contributed a lot to the Church and the society they were engaged with. Though "invisible" and "nameless wives" they worked for hand in hand with their husbands.[337] Were it not for their energetic and tireless support their husbands' works would have gone in vain.

Another book of Narola Imchen entitled Issues in Modern Historiography[338] is a feminist critique of Indian historiography, both secular and religious. In this book, Narola Imchen delineates how patriarchy is considered as the hub of female subordination. She proposes six elements that could alter patriarchal history such as dialogue, interpretation, context, asking questions (or being suspicious), social history and identification with the subject of study. She brings to notice the value of feminist historiography in appreciating women interest[339] and showing how partial history has been.

Santanu K. Patro's article, "The Dark Liberation in the Unpredictable, Untaming, Undying Kali: A Discourse on Dalit

---

[336] For details see Narola Imchen, *Remembering our Foremothers*, 239.

[337] See Narola Imchen, *Remembering our Foremothers*, 241, 242.

[338] Narola Imchen, *Issues in Modern Historiography* (Delhi: ISPCK, 2012). Hereafter cited as Narola Imchen, *Issues*.

[339] See Narola Imchen, *Issues*, 20-25.

Feminism in India"[340] gives a new reading of Kali[341] from feminist, subjugated perspective. In his article, Patro believes that even though Kali has been considered as cruel, castrating, and fearful goddess in history, she represents "power" which implies that women folks have power and that they can infuse gallantry and heroism in others especially among female members.[342] For him, the fact that Kali has been represented as terrifying gives room for grace and kindness. This is because she defeats fear and offers boon. "Kali is not the only boon giver and gracious, but also the healer of diseases by withholding death. Danger alone can counter danger."[343] This mode of re-interpretation is inspirational for Indian women.

Teresa Rehman's *The Mothers of Manipur: Twelve Women Who Made History*[344] is a collection of biographies of twelve Manipuri women who protested violent acts of Indian Army upon Manipur people, especially upon weaker female members. Teresa made it

---

[340] Santanu K. Patro, "The Dark Liberation in the Unpredictable, Untaming, Undying Kali: A Discourse on Dalit Feminism in India," in *Methodological Issues in Theological Research – An Exploration,* edited by H. Vanlalauva (Serampore: SATHRI, 2014), 39. Hereafter cited as Patro, "The Dark Liberation."

[341] Kali: (Sanskrit: "She Who Is Black" or "She Who Is Death") in Hinduism, goddess of time, doomsday, and death, or the black goddess (the feminine form of Sanskrit kala, "time-doomsday-death" or "black"). Kali's origins can be traced to the deities of the village, tribal, and mountain cultures of South Asia who were gradually appropriated and transformed, if never quite tamed, by the Sanskritic traditions. She makes her first major appearance in Sanskrit culture in the Devi Mahatmya ("The Glorifications of the Goddess," c. 6th century CE). Kali's iconography, cult, and mythology commonly associate her not only with death but also with sexuality, violence, and, paradoxically, in some later traditions, with motherly love. See Wendy Doniger, "Kali, Hindu Goddess," https://www.britannica.com/topic/Kali (27 July 2018).

[342] Ima Ibetombi, one of the women who took part in a nude protest in 2004 against the sexual violence of Indian Army on Manipuri female members confidently said, "If the police came forward we would have torn their pants and shirts. We were like goddess Kali – ready to devour," in Teresa Rehman, *The Mothers of Manipur – Twelve Women Who Made History* (New Delhi: Zubaan Publishers Private Limited, 2017), xix.

[343] Patro, "The Dark Liberation," 39.

[344] Teresa Rehman, *The Mothers of Manipur – Twelve Women Who Made History* (New Delhi: Zubaan Publishers Private Limited, 2017).

known to the world that even though these women are ordinary, literally vendors in Imphal's Ima Keithel (mother's market), they made history by taking part in a nude protest in 2004.

Summing up, feminist historiography opposes and deconstructs dominant patriarchy in history writing and offers critical re-evaluation that resists the patriarchal domination of women. In fact, in the past, Indian women were deprived of education and were even supposed to jump in their husband's funeral pyre which clearly showed the contemptible condition of Indian women in the past centuries. The physical condition as well as their role in the society had been pathetic.[345] Tackling the patriarchal hegemony inherent in India, the feminist historiography introduces emancipatory and liberatory aspects by visualizing a discipleship of equals where both sexes fight for liberation from male domination.[346] However, feminist historiography is not free from criticism. It fails to address the sufferings of women within the lower strata in the society. This can be attributed mostly to the feminist movement's obsession with sex and gender.

10.4.5. Innovative Trajectory of Tribal Historiography

Among all the different reasons that shaped the tribal historiography, the two Western agencies in the form of colonialism and Christian mission are accountable in a revolutionary role as well as in their life-renovating works. Since officers of the colonial rulers, administrators, and bureaucrats were legitimately appointed to preserve peace and order for the benefit of the British power, the history they wrote of tribal people in India was one of barbarism, inter-clan rivalry and savagism. This, according to their historiography, called for British intrusion in the region.[347]

---

[345] Kaholi Zhimomi, "Women during Armed Conflict: A Historical Re-reading of Indo-Naga Struggle in Nagaland from the Feminist Perspective" (D.Th dissertation, Senate of Serampore College, 2013).

[346] Rosy Zoramthangi, "Development of Methodological Trends," 42.

[347] For detailed elaboration see Vanlalpeka, "*Quo Vadis* Tribal Christian Historiography? A Study on the Historiography of Vanlalchhuanawma," unpublished paper, 1. Hereafter cited as Vanlalpeka, "*Quo Vadis* Tribal Christian Historiography?"

The offshoot of British historiography was felt when tribal Christian writers first attempted writing their own tribal history. Tribal writers, much inclined towards missionaries developed their historiography in religious worldview and what has stressed in their writings was that tribal culture was awaiting the arrival of Christianity in their lands for the reformation and redemption of their social, religious, and cultural lives. This holds true to a large extent at least from the titles of the books published concerning those times such as *From Head-hunting to Soul Hunting: An Account of Missionary Outreach of the Presbyterian Church in Mizoram,*[348] *From Head-hunting to the Hallelujah Chorus*[349] and the like.

The proposition that all cultural and historical practices pre-dating the advent of Christianity were preparatory in nature or simply animistic rituals in need of redemption is a widely held belief.[350] This notion posits that traditional practices and beliefs were fundamentally incomplete without the influence of Christianity. It implies that the introduction of Christianity served as a necessary step for the completion and perfection of these practices. This view has significant implications for the understanding of the impact of Christianity on traditional cultures, and has been the subject of much debate in academic and religious circles alike.

A shift from this paradigm took place with the appearance of postcolonial studies in the field of literature wherein tribal theology began to criticize colonial historiography and even tried to de-colonize the history of tribal Christianity. According to this historiography, missionaries, as well as colonizers, were alleged to have caused erosion of tribal culture in Northeast India by implanting a new, westernized way of life. For the tribal theologians, it is because of colonial rule in the area that peoples' minds are under British slavery. Tribal theology states that the introduction of Westernization and Christianity, because of British colonizers and missionaries, damaged the rich

[348] V. L. Zaithanga, *From Head-hunting to Soul-hunting: an Account of Missionary Outreach of the Presbyterian Church in Mizoram* (Aizawl: Synod Press, 1981).

[349] Katie Hughes *From Head-hunting to the Halleujah Chorus* (Aizawl: np, 1936).

[350] Vanlalpeka, "*Quo Vadis* Tribal Christian Historiography?" 1.

local social and cultural heritage of tribal people[351] and that Western Christianity dislodged traditional spiritual beliefs of tribal people. Thus, "the Christianity they came to practice was seen as part of a monolithic Western Christianity introduced by white missionaries… In such a view, people and their culture were looked upon as passive participants in the process of the historical encounter."[352]

But, after the 1990s, there is a new trajectory. Kipgen's book, *Christianity and Mizo Culture – The Encounter between Christianity and Zo Culture in Mizoram*[353] is one among this. Kipgen professes, "A limited knowledge of the Zo culture…led the earliest writers to dismiss the pre-modern Zos as "savages" who were not likely to change for the better. History has proved them wrong,"[354] and continues to say, "not only did the Zos adapt themselves to the changes that modernization brought to their area, but in the process, they created an identity that had many new elements but was deeply rooted in the cultural history of the people."[355] This interpretation shows that Mizos have their own way of resisting the new culture being brought to them by the Westerners and, that they have their own creative way of adaptation which suits their most inner-beings.

In the new historiographical trajectory, things continue to be twisted in a different course. Writers like Vanlalchhuanawma no longer embrace the idea that Westernization, along with colonialism shaped every bit of tribal peoples' worldview or influenced every piece of the tribal cultural trait. This philosophy is evidently seen

[351] See M. Thangkhosei Haokip, "The Impact of Christian Mission and British Colonialism among the Kuki People in Northeast India," http://kukiforum.com/2012/03/the-impact-of-christian-mission-and-british-colonialism-among-the-kuki-people-in-north-east-india/#_edn34 (13 Aug. 2018).

[352] B. L. Nongbri, "Change and Continuity – An Analysis of the Interaction of Khasi Traditional Religion with Christianity," in *Christianity in Indian History – Issues of Culture, Power and Knowledge,* edited by Pius Malekandathil, Joy L. K. Pachuau and Tanika Sarkar (Delhi: Primus Books, 2016), 58. Hereafter cited as B. L. Nongbri, "Change and Continuity."

[353] Mangkhosat Kipgen, *Christianity and Mizo Culture – The Encounter between Christianity and Zo Culture in Mizoram* (Jorhat: Mizo Theological Conference, 1997). Herafter cited as Kipgen, *Christianity and Mizo Culture.*

[354] Kipgen, *Christianity and Mizo Culture*, 313, 314.

[355] Kipgen, *Christianity and Mizo Culture*, 314.

in Vanlalchhuanawma's *Christianity and Subaltern Culture – Revival Movement as a Cultural Response to Westernization in Mizoram.*[356] That is to say, the tribals are not passive recipients of both the Gospel and Westernization. They do not candidly follow all they have been taught and they have their own way of either accepting or resisting the Gospel and the new culture being imposed on them.[357] This way of thinking developed in the late 1990s.

In the same vein, B. L. Nongbri, a tribal historian, articulates that the conversion of tribal into Christianity should not be elucidated in terms of colonial support since that view could lead to tribal being viewed as dumb and lacking consciousness.[358] He persuasively stated that tribal should not be seen as submissive partakers in the entire course of proselytization as "Christianity was not forced upon but adopted by the people who had their own agenda for doing so... this perspective attributes agency to the people and recognizes them as active participants who...shaped the events that affected their own history,"[359] which obviously marked the distinction of the new historiography from that of the previous ones.

10.4.6. Folklore as New Methodology for Writing of Social History in Northeast India

Discovering the history of the native community who certainly had a past but not a history is a discouraging job. The drawback lies in the fact that most of Northeast society was oral whereas the history writing depended heavily on printed works in black and white. In

---

[356] Vanlalchhuanawma, *Christianity and Subaltern Culture – Revival Movement as a Cultural Response to Westernization in Mizoram* (Delhi: ISPCK, 2006).

[357] Interview with Vanlalchhuanawma, former Principal of Aizawl Theological College, Aizawl and Union Biblical Seminary, Pune, 9th October, 2018.

[358] B. L. Nongbri, "Change and Continuity," 12.

[359] B. L. Nongbri's, "Christianity, Khasi Language and Literature: An Historical Analysis of the Interaction of Christianity with Traditional Culture," in T.B. Subba, Joseph Puthenpurakal and Shaji Joseph Puykunnel, eds, *Christianity and Change in Northeast India* (New Delhi: Concept Publishing Company, 2009), 12.

the face of the availability of scores of sources like archaeological, oral, and other accounts the colonial Western method of history writing underestimated earlier precious tales of the indigenous peoples[360] which categorically brings forth a dilemma for the native people who had been deprived of history on paper.

One valuable gift of the recent development in the trajectory of history writing is the re-definition of texts and sources. Because the Western notion of "text" suffers a sweeping change, oral sources come to occupy an essential place in providing a mine of information about the subjectivity of the past. As a result, legends, memories, fables, myths, stories, ballads, proverbs, folklores, and folksongs become "extra texts" for the historians,[361] which can be prudently and resolutely used for inventing the social, cultural, and religious history of Northeast India.

Thomas S. Szasz, a psychiatrist and academic markedly distinguished the divergence between animal empire and human empire in the following words: "In the animal kingdom, the rule is eat or be eaten; in the human kingdom, define or be defined."[362] This is hugely true of the history of Northeast India in the sense that Northeast peoples have been defined by outsiders while self-ascription of the people themselves remains missing.

A good illustration of how tribal peoples' own perception of themselves differs from the perception of the government is astonishingly given by V. V. Thomas. The following is a diagram of the misinterpreted views on tribals:[363]

---

[360] Malsawmdawngliana, *Negotiating the Past – Memory, History and Culture of Mizo* (Guwahati: Scientific Book Centre, 2015), 178.

[361] For detailed elaboration see Vanlalchhuanawma, "Methodological Issues in the Study of History of Christianity," 222.

[362] Thomas S. Szasz, *The Second Sin* (Garden City, New York: Anchor Press Doubleday and Company Inc., 1973), 20.

[363] V. V. Thomas, *Dalit and Tribal Christians*, 176.

Administrative Language	Tribal Language
Isolation in Forest	Casteless/Classless Egalitarian Society
Tribal Dialect	Community Bases Economic System
Animism	Symbolic With Nature
Primitive Occupation	Democratic Policy Based on Consensus
Carnivorous Diet	Fight for the Dignity and Right
Naked or Semi-naked	Change as per Demand of the Time and Climate
Nomadic Habits	Accommodative History
Love Drink and Dance	People-oriented Art and Literature

Against this backdrop, folklore is a significant resource for the writing of the history of the Northeastern region of India,[364] which is inhabited by more than 200 of the 635 tribal groups in India.[365] The people living in these areas have been identified, classified, and categorized by outside writers from the latter's perspectives, without acquiring deep knowledge of the indigenous peoples' identity and history. Therefore, the identity given to these people comes under the etic[366] notion of identity, and sadly not the emic[367] one. Since the history of Northeast India hitherto has been collected and put into writing by colonial administrators and Indian writers who do not

[364] Northeast India consists of eight sister states namely Assam, Arunachal Pradesh, Meghalaya, Mizoram, Manipur, Nagaland, Sikkim and Tripura.

[365] See Deka, "Folklore and Northeast Indian History," 4.

[366] An "etic" view of a culture is the perspective of an outsider looking in. See "Two Views of Culture: Etic and Emic," https://courses.lumenlearning.com/culturalanthropology/chapter/two-views-of-culture-etic-emic/ (21 Aug. 2018).

[367] An "emic" notion is an important tool of self-ascription that gives the people concerned their identity. See Joy L. K. Pachuau, "Mizo Identity Bihchianna" ("A Closer Scrutiny of Mizo Identity"), a paper presented on a joint seminar organized at Synod Conference Centre, Aizawl by SCMI: Aizawl Theological College Unit on 20th January, 2018.

belong to these dazzling upland regions, all we have about the area is a distorted, vague, and hazy history.

Throughout history, colonial administrators and white missionaries working in Northeast India have labelled Mizo and Naga tribes as head-hunters and the "dirtiest of all nations." However, who has the authority to apply such labels? In truth, it was not the Northeast Indian tribes who deserved such a title, but rather the British colonial rulers who caused countless bloodshed in their quest for new lands. The British were the real invaders and headhunters.

Unfortunately, this perspective has been missing from the methodology used to study the history of Northeast Indian societies. The problem with the current history we have is that it fails to give importance to the local peoples' own stories, experiences, folktales, and cultural heritage. Most written documents are either silent or prejudiced towards the religious and cultural aspects of these societies. As a result, the true story of these fascinating upland states has been misrepresented, misconstrued, and misunderstood by both Indian and non-Indian writers alike. To overcome these gaps in our understanding of history, it is necessary to turn to folklore as an important alternative source of information. By doing so, we can fill in the blanks and gain a better appreciation for the lives of these unique and captivating people.

Meeta Deka correctly penned down, thus, "Where there have been a dearth of written documents, archaeological and other evidence…folklore is significant to explain and understand societies in the context of preserving cultural diversity…"[368]

The difficulty of studying the history of Northeastern Indian people is added by the veracity that the region has larger resemblance and kinship in terms of geographical, race, culture, and tradition to its eastern neighbours like China, Tibet, Myanmar, and other Southeast Asian nations than with mainland India. This involuntarily led to an identity crisis as to whom these groups of people genuinely belong and the ethnic crisis makes the people

---

[368] Deka, "Folklore and Northeast Indian History," 1.

inquisitive to look for roots[369] and make up a history, in which folklore plays quite a significant role.

The colonial interpretation portrayed the role of evangelists and missionaries as the sole agent of religious change amongst the tribal and denounced indigenous worship as devilish and as having a connection with evil spirits, cannibalism, and animism. That much is what white peoples' interpretation put in the picture. On the contrary, if one looks circumspectly at the folk stories, tales, and songs of the indigenous communities one can discover that there were elements of the fear of God, sincerity, earnestness, and genuineness on the part of the worshippers. There was a time when a tribal group had face to face interaction with God.[370] This leads us to the conclusion that the tribal communities accepted Jesus Christ, not because of outward factors like the coming of missionaries, but because God dwells in their heart and that God spoke to them and enthused them to believe in Jesus Christ, whosoever the agent might be. This facet of tribal religiosity can be rediscovered from a genuine study of tribal folklore.

10.5. Where do We Go from Here?

Having examined the different historiographies of Christianity in India, it is evident that one set of historiographical tools is kind of inept to integrate all spheres of the community as well as individual lives. What kind of historiography we are supposed to envision is a question every serious historian is now faced with.

Firstly, a more spacious version of the postcolonial historiography needs to be thought of. In other words, the new historiography which is not confined to the framework of anti-colonial and anti-missionary oratory only is needed[371] since the de-construction of colonialism has been done in large quantity for a long time already. To formulate a new way of history writing, U. R.

---

[369] For detailed elaboration see Deka, "Folklore and Northeast Indian History," 4.

[370] See V. Lunghnema, *Mizo Chronicles: Mizo Hun Kal Zela Thil Thleng Chhinchhiahna 4000 BC – AD 1976* (Churachandpur: H. Zairema, 1994), 7.

[371] See C. I. David Joy, *Overlooked Voices – A Postcolonial Indian Quest* (USA, Borderless Press, 2015), 130. Hereafter cited as David Joy, *Overlooked Voices.*

Ananthamurthy proposes that global worries, concerns, and literary works need to be translated and apprehended within the clearer framework of native cultures and languages.[372] The importance of taking the indigenous culture or going after the ethnographic line is also distinctly expressed by Pheme Perkins in the following words:[373]

> As third world Christians emerge from the hegemony of European imperialism, they are discovering patterns of meaning and coherence appropriate to their communal experience. Although Western readers frequently speak of Asian theology as though it derived from a single cultural tradition, such a generalization says more about European hegemony than about the cultures involved.

This clearly shows that the indigenous peoples' cultures are not given enough consideration and that they are taken for granted for a long time. Therefore, acknowledging the presence of distinct and divergent cultures, a historiography along the cultural and the ethnic lines is visualized so that people from different cultures may have their fair share of space in the new historiography. This may hopefully minimize the use of derogative terms like tribal, dalits etc. in addressing these distinct, intrinsic and unique communities.

Secondly, an alternative historiography in lieu of postcolonial theory may be proposed with historical resistance motifs. According to Bhambra, "postcolonial historiography has nonetheless reproduced some equivalent hierarchies in its own representation of history from the point of view of the subaltern."[374] It is obvious that there is a very little or no serious effort from the point of view of the theological academy to recognize both history writing and the biblical interpretation in the native language by theologians in the colonial as well as postcolonial periods. This is mainly because only literature in the English language could be recognized at the global

---

[372] As cited by David Joy, *Overlooked Voices*, 150.

[373] Pheme Perkins, "Canon, Paradigms and Progress? Reflections on the Essays by Rendtorff, Sugirtharajah and Clines," in *Biblical Interpretation* 1/1, 1993, 89.

[374] J. Jayakiran Sebastian, *Enlivening the Past: an Asian Theologian's Engagement with the Early Teachers of Faith* (Piscataway, NJ: Gorgias Press, 2009), 6.

level.[375] Furthermore, most of the postcolonial discourses are done in English, which has a "universal mission." However, "the biblical focus on mission is always to uphold the people on the edges and at the margins by proffering them an ambiance of justice and peace,"[376] which necessitates the use of vernacular language in history writing. If we really care for the well-being and development of native people, we should give a solemn attempt so that they understand the historical and theological discourses in their own mother tongue.

Thirdly, it seems true that the subaltern historiography fails to cover all aspects of the problems of subaltern masses as there are undoubtedly various subaltern groups which the subaltern historiography could not deal with. This holds true of the feminist historiography, too. Speaking of women's ascendancy towards lower women, Jacquelyn Grant compellingly penned down the following words:[377]

> Black women, as part of the servicing class, were not awarded the protection of White patriarchy...Brutality was administered not only by masters and foremen but also by mistresses, reflecting the fact that White women were just as much participants in the system of slavery as were White men.

Women have been oppressing women, which is where the problem with feminist gender concerns lies. As the term "feminist" is disparaged for its exclusiveness in the context of human sexuality and gender issues, a more inclusive term "Womanist"[378] which refers

---

[375] See David Joy, *Overlooked Voices*, 128.

[376] David Joy, *Overlooked Voices*, 128.

[377] As cited by David Joy, *Overlooked Voices*, 144.

[378] "Womanist" historiography or womanist theology is an emergent voice of African American Christian women in the United States. Employing Alice Walker's definition of womanism in her text In Search of Our Mothers' Garden, black women in America are calling into question their suppressed role in the African American church, the community, the family, and the larger society. See Linda E. Thomas, "Womanist Theology, Epistemology, and a New Anthropological Paradigm," http://www.crosscurrents.org/thomas.htm (7 Oct. 2018).

to the experiences and struggles faced by African-American, Latino, Asian, Dalits, and Tribal come to be employed in recent times.

Therefore, a task ahead of us is more than mere de-construction of male domination in history. Rather, it is the construction of a theology which includes interrogating the social construction of depressed (black, Dalits, Tribal, etc.) womanhood in relation to their concerned communities and to assume a liberatory perspective so disheartened and dejected women can live emboldened lives[379] within their communities as well as in a broader context.

Consequently, departing from feminist historiography, "womanist historiography" will occupy more prominent part in the years to come because of the failure of feminist historiography to tackle the everyday realities of women of colour as well as the depressed classes and the lack of understanding of the full dimension of liberation from the unique oppressions of black, dalit and tribal women. In this discourse, the "experience" of suffering and oppressed women from varied backgrounds will serve a meaningful purpose.

Fourthly, a "diasporic historiography," which gives primacy to the movement of the people – migration and communities who are always at the margins – can boldly be envisaged to take more attention in the times to come. This gives precedence to the questions of race and ethnicity, which are never fixed and given but are rather always in the process of formation, interconnecting and overlapping with notions of class, nation, sexuality, colonialism and, empire.[380] This history helps in appreciating various cultures, breaching the barriers between different cultures and countries, g/localizing the global and spreading words of worldwide peaçe. As migration inrush and influx increase and as the sense of homelessness suffered by immigrants is deep and intense, this kind of history writing will obtain a more noticeable place in history writing. This writing searches the hunt for

---

[379] Lind E. Thomas, "Womanist Theology, Epistemology, and a New Anthropological Paradigm," http://www.crosscurrents.org/thomas.htm (5 Oct. 2018).

[380] DJA Clines, "Contemporary Methods in Hebrew Bible Criticism", in *Hebrew Bible Old Testament: The History of Its Interpretation III/2 The 20th Century,* ed by Magne Saebo (Gottingen: Vandenhoeck & Ruprecht Gmbh & Co, 2015): 166.

identity, uprooting and re-rooting, insider and outsider syndrome and nostalgia and sentimentality.

10.6. Concluding Appraisal

The transition of Indian Christian historiography in the first historical narrative was not significant as during that time history writing was dominated by imperial hegemony. The most perceptible historiography presented by colonial writers was India was backward in every sphere of life and this fact called for white peoples' intervention in the area. The Oriental despotism on the part of the administrators gave way for the British to present the British government in India as the medium in changing the alleged corrupted Indian society. That was to the British the *raison d'être* of the British rule of India. Justification and validation of the British Indian government occupied the core imperial historiography.

The same stance was brought in by evangelists and missionaries who presented the history of Christianity in India as another room of Western Christianity which is nothing but an extension of Western Christianity in a foreign land that is India. Stories of missionaries are told in such a way that they were conquerors, leading actors, warriors, and heroes in their missionary enterprises whereas native contributions have been either silenced or sidelined in the accounts of the history of Christianity. "Missionaries saw their work as transformative, transforming the "primitive" to the "modern," the "savage" to the "civilized," and this was accomplished not only through education, health care, but also the moral and ethical ethos that Christianity was seen to have produced."[381] Besides this, what is arresting in the colonial and missionary historiography is that it was hugely male-oriented.

A fresh trajectory showed up in the form of nationalist historiography which contradicted and counteracted colonial historiography. This was really a turning point in the history of Christianity in India. On one hand, the nationalist historiography

[381] Joy L. K. Pachuau, "Post-colonialism and the Writing of the History of Christianity," an unpublished paper. Hereafter cited as Joy L. K. Pachuau, "Post-colonialism."

unearthed Indian past glory which was left out by colonizers. Indian political, cultural, and social glory had been rediscovered through this new historiography, albeit romanticization took place in some writers' conversations with the past. In fact, it was this nationalist history that inflamed Indian nationals to have upbeat and cheery feelings towards their motherland. On the other hand, nationalist historiography had the inclination towards a pro-Hindu nation which mechanically counts out and rejects all other religious institutions. What is more, this new form of historiography projected only those persons who were taking the leading role in the nationalist movement thus it automatically dropped off the history of the subalterns in the freedom movement.

To smoothen the pioneering trajectory launched by nationalist historiography the CHAI Historiography jumped in with a view to challenging missionaries' ecclesiastical history as well as to writing history from an indigenous perspective. This was again a watershed in the study of the history of Christianity in India. At the same time, the new path followed by the CHAI also had its own snags and drawbacks. Majority of the writers of CHAI history books are not Indians even though they spent much of their time in India. A pertinent question is whether they genuinely feel the anguish of poverty-stricken Indians especially of the lower strata of the society who constitute the majority of Christians in India.

In the multi-volumes of CHAI history produced so far, a very important source, i.e., the oral source is not given prominent importance. The oral source is invaluable to meaningfully study the history of Dalits and Tribal. This important source is not consulted by most writers of the CHAI-Volumes except for Hugald Grafe's, *History of Christianity in India: Tamil Nadu in the Nineteenth and Twentieth Centuries.*[382] *CHAI needs to take serious note of this for the upcoming publications.*

The CHAI needs careful consideration not to engage itself in dominant, denominational historiography, albeit it takes efforts to produce socio-historical and ecumenical history. "What is needed in

[382] Grafe, *History of Christianity in India: Tamil Nadu in the Nineteenth and Twentieth Centuries*, 300.

the historiographical tool is a space for the local authors where they can write their own history, in their own perspective, for their own people."[383] Since the books published hitherto are lacking authors who can write from indigenous, subaltern perspectives, the need of the hour is the employment of writers from the subaltern group of people who can produce history on behalf of the overlooked, voiceless, and neglected sections of the Indian society.

Another important transition took place with the initiation of Postcolonial historiography which surfaced after Independence. In principle, postcolonial theory is not a theory since it does not put forward a unified set of dogma, nor does it have a single author. It is a perspective that surfaced in a body of literature to oppose dictatorial relations by the West.[384] Needless to say here that postcolonialism cannot be identified as a period that started only after independence because it impinges on the societies of the postcolonial world from the opening of colonization up to this day. Under postcolonial studies, various new trajectories find their inventive ways such as subaltern, feminist, Dalits, Tribal, so on and so forth. Nevertheless, there is still a long way to go. To cite one example, though subaltern historians can theorize communalism, they are still unable to speak with ease about religion or the supernatural not because of the negligence of rational principles but by its dominance. This necessitates the liberation of subaltern writers even after subaltern writings seem to make their appearance in the history of secular as well as Christianity in India.

Succinctly, Historiography of Christianity in India has undergone momentous changes and transitions within the last two hundred or more years. Remarkably and captivatingly, there are new trajectories too. The first and foremost transition was seen in the historians and the people concerned in this venture. In the nineteenth century, most of the historians, publishers and intended readers of the books published were Western people. Protestant and Roman Catholic histories dominated the entire scene in general history. During the twentieth century, Indians came to be

---

[383] A-a, "Historiographical Tools," 34.

[384] Joy L. K. Pachuau, "Post-colonialism," 1,2.

seen as history writers as well as anticipated readers.[385] Startlingly, after the 1960s, the Indian Christian historiography takes a more engaging trajectory. Historians and projected readers not only include Indian Christians, but also people of other faith traditions. Astonishingly, Hindus and Muslims started taking up Indian Christian history as their doctoral dissertation and whose intended readers also are outside of the Christian fold. This wider range of aims and perspectives confront every serious historian of Indian Christianity to consider it as a challenge and take positive measures. The Churchly obsessions and concerns of the nineteenth century (Protestant versus Catholic; Church and state; missionary methods; Padroado versus Propaganda) over and above the twentieth century (the indigenization, unity, mission of the Indian Church) are not the lone concerns and topics of historians and their readers as they once were. With the augmentation of the social and scholarly framework in which the history of Christianity in India is now written swells the complications that historians must face in selecting a suitable method of research. Consequently, a fine historian has to keep this broader social and intellectual context in mind in presenting the history of Christianity in India. Appreciably, after the 1960s, the readership has been transferred from Christians to Hindus and Muslims, albeit Christians form a majority in the readership faction.[386]

During the last few decades, history writing lays more stress on social, economic, and cultural processes, giving attention to local areas which have the tendency to be nationalistic in nature.[387] From the 1980s onwards, a fresher transition appeared especially in the writing of conversion movements among Dalits and Tribal people. In earlier historiography, the "whys" of the conversion movement was credited to the Divine. In the new trajectory, there is a trend which searches out pre-Christian Dalit and Tribal religiosity which could be accessed to make Christianity recognizable. History is written

---

[385] For detailed elaboration see John C.B. Webster, *Historiography,* 59, 60.

[386] See John C. B. Webster, *Historiography,* 60.

[387] Sangkima, "R. Vanlawma," in *Historians and Historiography of Northeast India,* edited by J. B. Bhattacherjee (New Delhi: Akansha Publishing House, 2012), 190.

from the perspective of self-expression and agency. A question began to be asked if missionaries really comprehended native culture and characteristics. Indigenous communities are deemed custodians of Christianity and missionary interpretation of the faith was instead questioned. "Agency in practice and understanding was appropriated by…themselves and in the process, Christianity became localized and vernacularized."[388]

The present document draws to a close, but it does not signify the termination of the unceasing, perennial, and ceaseless trajectories of historiography. The study of history is an indispensable pursuit that educates, enlightens, and enriches the human intellect. It is a discipline that calls for continuous exploration, examination, and analysis of the past to make sense of the present and envision a better future. As such, it requires our unwavering attention, devotion, and commitment to the pursuit of knowledge.

---

[388] Joy L. K. Pachuau, ""Post-colonialism," 8, 9.

Bibliography

Books

Ashcroft, Bill, Gareth Griffiths, Helen Tiffin. *The Empire Writes Back: Theory and Practice in Postcolonial Literatures.* New York: Routledge, 1989.

Avis, Paul. *Foundations of Modern Historical Thought: From Machiavelli to Vico.* London: Croom Helm Ltd., 1986.

Barraclough, Geoffrey. *History in a Changing World.* England: Oxford Blackwell, 1955.

Bebbington, David. *Patterns in History.* Leicester: InterVarsity Press, 1979.

Bhasin, Kamla, Nighat Said Khan. *Some Questions on Feminism and its Relevance in South Asia.* Reprint. New Delhi: Kali for Women, 2000.

Bradley, James E., Richard A. Muller. *Church History: An Introduction to Research Methods and Resources.* 2nd ed. Grand Rapids, Cambridge: William B. Eerdmans Publishing Company, 2016.

Carr, E. H. *What is History?* England: Penguin Books, 1961.

Carr, E. H. *What is History?* Reprinted. Harmondsworth, Middlesex, England, Penguin Books Ltd, 1981.

Cantor, Norman F., Richard I Schneider. *How to Study History.* Arlington Heights, Illinois: A.H.M. Publishing Corporation, 1967.

Chakrabarty, Dipesh. *Provincializing Europe – Postcolonial Thought and Historical Difference.* New Delhi: Oxford University Press, 2001.

Chitnis, K. N. *Research Methodology in History.* 4th ed. New Delhi: Atlantic Publishers and Distributors Pvt Ltd., 2023.

Cohen, M. R., Ernest Nagel, *An Introduction to Logic and Scientific Method.* London: Routledge and Kegan Paul Ltd., 1934.

Collingwood, R. G. *The Idea of History.* Revised ed. New York: Oxford University Press, 2007.

Daughrity, Dyron B. *The Changing World of Christianity – the Global History of a Borderless Religion.* New York, Peter Lang Publishing Incorporation, 2010.

Downs, Frederick S. *History of Christianity in India: North East India in the Nineteenth and Twentieth Centuries.* Volume V, Part 5. Bangalore: The Church History Association of India, 2003.

D'Sa, M. *History of the Catholic Church in India, Vol. I: A.D. 52-1652.* Bombay: The Lalka Printing and Litho Works, 1910.

D'Sa, M. *History of the Catholic Church in India, Vol. II: A.D. 1652-1924.* Bombay: The Lalka Printing and Litho Works, 1924.

Dubois, Abbe J. A., Henry K. Beauchamnp. *Hindu Manners, Customs and Ceremonies.* London: Clarendon Press, 1906.

Dutt, Romesh Chunder. *A History of Civilization in Ancient India.* Calcutta: Thacker, Spink & Co., 1891.

Dutt, Romesh Chunder. *Early Hindu Civilization.* 4th ed. Calcutta: Punthipustak, 1963.

Eliade, Mircea. *Images and Symbols: Studies in Religious Symbolism.* London: Harvill Press, 1961.

Elton, G. R. *The Practice of History.* Glasgow: William Collin's Sons and Co. Ltd., 1979.

Ferro, Marc. *The Use and Abuse of History.* London, New York: Routledge, 2012.

Fridlund, M., M. Oiva, & P. Paju (Eds.) *Digital Histories: Emergent Approaches within the New Digital History.* Helsinki: Helsinki University Press, 2020.

Guha, Ranajit. *An Indian Historiography of India: A Nineteenth Century Agenda and Its Implications.* Calcutta: Centre for Studies in Social Science, 1988.

Guha, Ranajit. *Elementary Aspects of Peasant Insurgency in Colonial India.* Durham: Duke University Press, 1999.

Hambye, E. R. *History of Christianity in India: Eighteenth Century.* Volume III. Bangalore: The Church History Association of India, 1997.

Harvey, Van A. *The Historian and the Believer.* Bloomsbury Street, London: S.C.M. Press Ltd, 1967.

Hirst, Paul Q. *Marxism and Historical Writing.* New York: Routledge, 2017.

Hough, James. *Informations and Suggestions for the Use of Missionaries, Missionary Candidates and Committees.* London: Hatchard and Son, 1832.

Houpert, Joseph C. S. J. *A South Indian Mission: the Madura Catholic Mission from 1535 to 1935.* New ed. Trichinopoly: St. Joseph's Industrial School Press, 1937.

Hughes, H. Stuart. *History as Art and as Science: Twin Vistas on the Past.* New York: Harper and Row, 1964.

Hughes, Katie. *From Head-hunting to the Halleujah Chorus.* Aizawl: np, 1936.

Iggers, Georg G., Edward Wang. *A Global History of Modern Historiography.* Noida: Dorling Kindersley, 2010.

Imchen, Narola. *Issues in Modern Historiography.* Delhi: I.S.P.C.K., 2012.

Imchen, Narola. *Remembering our Foremothers – the Influence of the American Women's Movement on American Baptist Women Missionaries in Northeast India.* Jorhat: Women Study Department, E.T.C., 2003.

Jain, Laxmi. *Historical Method and Historiography.* New Delhi: Vayu Education of India, 2016.

James, Woba. *Major Issues in the History of Christianity in India: A Post Colonial Reading.* Jorhat: T.D.C.C., 2013.

Joy, C. I. David. *Overlooked Voices – A Postcolonial Indian Quest.* U.S.A., Borderless Press, 2015.

Jordan, Z. A. *The Evolution of Dialectical Materialism: A Philosophical and Sociological Analysis.* London: Macmillan, 1967.

Khurana, K. L. *Concepts and Methods of Historiography.* 8th ed. Agra: Lakhsmi Narain Agarwal, 2017.

Kipgen, Mangkhosat. *Christianity and Mizo Culture – The Encounter between Christianity and Zo Culture in Mizoram.* Jorhat: Mizo Theological Conference, 1997.

Ludden, David. Ed. *Reading Subaltern Studies: Critical Histories, Contested Meaning and the Globalization of South Asia.* Delhi: Permanent Black, 2002.

Lunghnema, V. *Mizo Chronicles: Mizo Hun Kal Zela Thil Thleng Chhinchhiahna 4000 BC – AD 1976.* Churachandpur: H. Zairema, 1994.

Mabry, Hunter P. *A Manual for Researchers and Writers of Course Assignments, Theses, Dissertations, and Other Research Reports.* 2nd ed. Bangalore: B.T.E.S.S.C., 2011.

Majoros, Sotirios. *All About Me: The Individual.* Victoria, Canada: Friesen Press, 2019.

Malsawmdawngliana. *Negotiating the Past – Memory, History and Culture of Mizo.* Guwahati: Scientific Book Centre, 2015.

Marius, Richard, Melvin E. Page. *A Short Guide to Writing About History.* 7th ed. New York: Pearson Education Inc, 2010.

Marwick, Arthur. *The Nature of History.* London: Macmillan Press, 1970.

Marwick, Arthur. *The Nature of History.* 4th ed. London: Macmillan Press Ltd, 1979.

Morley, Neville. *Writing Ancient History.* New Delhi: Bloomsbury, 1999.

Mundadan, A. M., C.M.I. *History and Beyond.* Kerala: Jeevass Publications, 1997.

Mundadan, A. M. *History of Christianity in India, Vol I: From the Beginning up to the Middle of the Sixteenth Century.* Bangalore: CHAI, 1989.

Rajayyan, K. *Historiography: History in Theory and Method.* Madurai: Madurai Publishing House, 1976.

Rehman, Teresa. *The Mothers of Manipur – Twelve Women Who Made History.* New Delhi: Zubaan Publishers Private Limited, 2017.

Sharma, R. S., *Rethinking India's Past.* New Delhi: Oxford University Press, 2009.

Sherring, M. A. *The History of Protestant Missions in India, from their Commencements in 1706 to 1871.* London: Trubner and Co., 1875.

Sebastian, J. Jayakiran. *Enlivening the Past: An Asian Theologian's Engagement with the Early Teachers of Faith.* Piscataway, N.J.: Gorgias Press, 2009.

Spivak, Gayatri Chakravorty. *A Critique of Postcolonial Reason: Toward a History of the Vanishing Present.* Cambridge, Massachussets: Harvard University Press, 1999.

Sreedharan, E. *A Textbook of Historiography - 500 BC to AD 2000.* Reprint. New Delhi: Orient Blackswan, 2014.

Szasz, Thomas S. *The Second Sin.* Garden City, New York: Anchor Press Doubleday and Company Inc., 1973.

Thekkedath, Joseph. *History of Christianity in India: From the Middle of the Sixteenth Century to the End of the Seventeenth Century (1542 – 1700).* Volume II. Bangalore: Church History Association of India, 2001.

Thomas, V. V. *Dalit and Tribal Christians of India – Issues and Challenges.* Malapuram: Focus India Trust, 2014.

Thompson, Edward. *The Other Side of the Medal.* London: Hogarth Press, 1925.

Thompson, James Westfall. *A History of Historical Writing Volume II: the Eighteenth and Nineteenth Centuries.* 3rd ed. New York: Macmillan Company, 1954.

Trible, Phyllis. *God and the Rhetoric of Sexuality.* Philadelphia: Fortress Press, 1978.

Tungoe, Merithung. *Administrators Missionaries and a World Turned Upside Down.* Delhi: ISPCK, 2000.

Upadhyay, Shashi Bhushan. *Historiography in the Modern World – Western and Indian Perspectives.* New Delhi: Oxford University Press, 2016.

Vanlalchhuanawma. *Christianity and Subaltern Culture – Revival Movement as a Cultural Response to Westernization in Mizoram.* Delhi: I.S.P.C.K., 2006.

Webster, John C. B. *An Introduction to History.* 2nd ed. Delhi: Macmillan, 1981.

Webster, John C. B. *Historiography of Christianity in India.* 2nd ed. New Delhi: Oxford University Press, 2014.

Webster, John C. B. *Studying History.* Reprinted. Delhi: Macmillan, 2006.

Will, Ariel Durant. *The Lessons of History.* Bombay: Mohan Punjabi Hans Publishers, 1977.

Wilson, Norman J. *History in Crisis – Recent Directions in Historiography.* 3rd ed. U.S.A.: Pearson, 2014.

Zaithanga, V. L. *From Head-hunting to Soul-hunting: an Account of Missionary Outreach of the Presbyterian Church in Mizoram.* Aizawl: Synod Press, 1981.

Articles on Books

Alam, Javeed. "Peasantry, Politics and Historiography: Critique of New Trend in Relation to Marxism." In *Reading Subaltern Studies:*

Critical Histories, Contested Meaning and the Globalization of South Asia. Edited by David Ludden. Delhi: Permanent Black, 2002.

Arnold, David. "Subaltern Studies – Then and Now." In *New Subaltern Politics – Reconceptualizing Hegemony and Resistance in Contemporary India.* Edited by Alf Gunvald Niolsen, Srila Roy. New Delhi: Oxford University Press, 2015.

Basham, A. L. "Modern Historians of Ancient India." In *Historians of India, Pakistan and Ceylon.* Edited by C.H. Philips (London: Oxford University Press, 1977.

Butterfield. "Historiography." *Dictionary of History of Ideas.* Edited by Wiener, Philip Paul. Vol. 2. Minnesota: Scribner, 1973.

Chaudhuri, B. B. "Subaltern Autonomy and the National Movement." In *Reading Subaltern Studies: Critical Histories, Contested Meaning and the Globalization of South Asia.* Edited by David Ludden. Delhi: Permanent Black, 2002.

Clines, D. J. A. "Contemporary Methods in Hebrew Bible Criticism." In *Hebrew Bible Old Testament: The History of Its Interpretation III/2 The 20th Century.* Edited by Magne Saebo. Gottingen: Vandenhoeck & Ruprecht Gmbh & Co, 2015.

Das, Veena. "Subaltern as Perspective." In *Subaltern Studies VI – Writings on South Indian History and Society.* Edited by Ranajit Guha. New Delhi: Oxford University Press, 1992.

Fischhoff, Baruch. "For Those Condemned to Study the Past: Heuristics and Biases in Hindsight." In *Judgment Under Uncertainty: Heuristics and Biases.* Edited by Kahneman, Daniel, Paul Slovic, Mos Tversky. Cambridge, U.K.: Cambridge University Press, 1982.

Florovsky, Georges. "The Predicament of the Christian Historian." In *God, History and Historians: An Anthology of Modern Christian Views of History.* Edited by McIntire. New York: Oxford University Press, 1977.

Gordon, A. D., et al. "The problem of Women's History." In *Liberating Women's History: Theoretical and Critical Essays.* Edited by Bernice A. Carroll. Urbana: University of Illinois Press, 1976.

Gruchy, John W. De. "Who Did They Think They Were – Some Reflections from a Theologian on Grand Narratives and Identity in the History of Missions." In *The Imperial Horizons of British Protestant Missions, 1880-1914.* Edited by Andrew Porter. Grand Rapids, Michigan: William B. Eerdmans Publishing Company, 2003.

Guha, Ranajit. "On Some Aspects of the Historiography." In *Subaltern Studies I: Writings on South Asian History and Society.* Edited by Ranajit Guha. New Delhi: Oxford University Press, 1982.

Lang, Sean. "The First Year Experience." In *History Skills – A Student's Handbook.* Edited by Mary Abbott. 3rd ed. London: Routledge, 2009.

McClintock, Anne. "The Angel of Progress: Pitfalls of the Term Postcolonialism." In *Colonial Discourse/Postcolonial Theory.* Edited by Francis Barker, Peter Hulme and Margaret Iversen. New Delhi: Viva Books, 2012.

Nongbri, B. L. "Change and Continuity – An Analysis of the Interaction of Khasi Traditional Religion with Christianity." In *Christianity in Indian History – Issues of Culture, Power and Knowledge.* Edited by Pius Malekandathil, Joy L. K. Pachuau and Tanika Sarkar. Delhi: Primus Books, 2016.

Nongbri, B. L. "Christianity, Khasi Language and Literature: An Historical Analysis of the Interaction of Christianity with Traditional Culture." In *Christianity and Change in Northeast India.* Edited by T. B. Subba, Joseph Puthenpurakal and Shaji Joseph Puykunnel. New Delhi: Concept Publishing Company, 2009.

Patro, Santanu K. "The Dark Liberation in the Unpredictable, Untaming, Undying Kali: A Discourse on Dalit Feminism in India." In *Methodological Issues in Theological Research – An Exploration.* Edited by H. Vanlalauva. Serampore: S.A.T.H.R.I., 2014.

Pushparajan, A. "A Secular Critique of Hindutva." In *Hindutva: An Indian Christian Response.* Edited by J. Mattam, S.J., P. Arockiadoss, S.J. Bangalore: Dharmaram Publications, 2002.

Puthenpurackal, Johnson. "History as the Story of Victors: A Postmodern Reading." In *History and Historizing: Philosophical Reflections.* Edited by John Peter Vallabadoss. Bangalore: Asian Trading Corporation, 2012.

Ralte, Lalfakawma. "Mizo Hnam Tobul, Kan Zik Chhuahna leh Kan Pem Kualna." In *Mizo Identity Bihchianna.* Edited by B. Lalnunzira. Aizawl: SCMI, ATC Unit, 2019.

Roberts, Michael. "The Annales School and Historical Writing." In *Making History: An Introduction to the History and Practices of a Discipline.* Edited by Peter Lambert and Phillipp Schofield.

Sangkima. "R. Vanlawma." In *Historians and Historiography of Northeast India.* Edited by J. B. Bhattacherjee. New Delhi: Akansha Publishing House, 2012.

Sen, Sunil. "Romesh Chandra Dutt." In *Historians and Historiography in Modern India.* Edited by S. P. Sen. Calcutta: Institute of Historical Studies, 1973.

Snaitang, O. L. "From Church History to History of Christianity - Historiographical Issues in the Study of Missiology in India." In *Mission and Evangelism.* Edited by Somen Das. Delhi: ISPCK, 1998.

Thanzauva, K. "Methodological Issues – Subaltern Perspectives." In *Methodological Issues in Theological Research – an Exploration.* Edited by H. Vanlalauva. Serampore: SATHRI, 2014.

Thomas, V. V. "A Survey of the Recent Historiographical Developments in India Including that of the Dalit and Tribal Movements." In *Methodological Issues in Theological Research – An Exploration.* Edited by H. Vanlalauva. Serampore: Department of Research/SATHRI, 2014.

Vanlalchhuanawma. "Methodological Issues in the Study of History of Christianity." In *Methodological Issues in Theological Research –*

An Exploration. Edited by H. Vanlalauva. Serampore: Department of Research/SATHRI, 2013.

Walotemjen. "Methodological Issues and Historiography of Christianity in India." In *Mapping the Context: An Interdisciplinary Exploration.* Edited by Imsenperong, Menjiwopong Jamir and Walotemjen. np: the Authors, 2011.

Articles on Journals

"Editorial." In *Indian Church History Review.* I/1 (June, 1967): 1.

Chatterjee, Margareth. "The Meaning of History: Principal Miller Endowment Lecture." In *Journal of the Madras University*, XLVII/2 (July, 1976): 1-17.

Fischhoff, Baruch. "Hindsight not Equal to Foresight: The Effect of Outcome Knowledge on Judgment Under Uncertainty." In *Journal of Experimental Psychology: Human Perception and Performance.* Vol. 1 (1975): 288-299.

Harbold, W. "Progressive Humanity: In the Philosophy of P. J. Proudhon," In *The Review of Politics,* 31/1: 28-47.

Hedlund, Roger E. "Approaches to Indian Church History in Light of New Christian Movements." In *Indian Church History Review.* 34/2 (December 2000): 150-176.

"Historiography." In *The Shorter Oxford English Dictionary on Historical Principles.* Edited by C. T. Onions. 3rd ed. Oxford: Clarendon Press, ny: 906.

"Historiography." In *Oxford Advanced Learner's Dictionary.* Edited by Hey, Leonie, Suzanne Holloway. United Kingdom: Oxford University Press, (2015): 743-745.

Inden, Ronald. "Orientalist Constructions of India." In *Modern Asian Studies* 20/3 (1986): 440-465.

Mundadan, A. M. "Changing Approaches to Historiography." In *Indian Church History Review.* 35/1 (June, 2001): 50-67.

Naidu, H. Gowri. "Philosophy of History." In *JETIR,* 1/6, (November 2014): 1560-1572.

Perkins, Pheme. "Canon, Paradigms and Progress? Reflections on the Essays by Rendtorff, Sugirtharajah and Clines." In *Biblical Interpretation.* 1/1, 1993.

Rao, Potana Venkateswara. "Christian Historiography: Changing Perspectives and Approaches in the Study of Christianity in India." In *Global Journal for Research Analysis.* 3/7 (July, 2014): 140-159.

Trible, Phyllis. "Depatriachalizing in Biblical Interpretation." In *JAAR.* 41 (1973): 30-48.

Wilfred, Felix. "Historiography of Indian Christianity, Some Reflections." In *Vidyjyoti.* 73/10 (October, 2009): 10-25.

Vanlalchhuanawma. "History leh Ziak Dan Thar Lo Chhuah Dan." (History and the Development of New Style of Writing) In *Didakhe.* 56/2 (March-April, 2017): 4-15.

Online Materials

"Auguste Comte Positivism." www.studyandexam.com/comte-positivism.html (6 Sept. 2023).

"Cultural History." http://www.encyclopedia.com/history/dictionaries-thesauruses-pictures-and-press-releases/cultural-history (6 April 2024).

"Historical Bias." https://www.boundless.com/world-history/textbooks/boundless-world-history-textbook/ (21 Sept. 2023).

"History as Art or Science." https//:owlcation.com/humanities/History-Art-or-Science (17 July 2023).

"History is Just One Damn Thing after Another." https://quoteinvestigator.com/2015/09/16/history/ (10 Aug. 2018).

"Types of Sources and Where to Find Them: Secondary Sources." https://www.library.illinois.edu/hpnl/tutorials/secondary-sources (21 Sept. 2023).

"What are the 10 Different Sources of Information?" https://edupepper.com/what-are-the-10-different-sources-of-information/ (20 Sept. 2023).

"What are the Differences?" https://crk.umn.edu/library/primary-secondary-and-tertiary-sources (20 Sept. 2023).

"What does Mr. Gradgrind say is the most important philosophy?" https://www.enotes.com/homework-help/what-does-mr-gradgrind-say-is-the...(18 Sept. 2023).

"What is a Primary Source." https://guides.library.harvard.edu/HistSciInfo/primary (19 Sept. 2023).

"What is Feminist Historiography in Detail?" https://brainly.in/question/4567790 (5 Oct. 2018).

"What is Literary Source?" https://edurev.in/question/3095891/ (19 Sept. 2023).

"What was Vico's cyclical idea of history?" ebrary.net/5101/philosophy/vicos_cyclical_idea_history (ebrary.net) (6 Sep 2023).

Abbenhuis, Maartje. "The Present as History." *The Present as History - Fifteen Eightyfour.* Cambridge University Press (cambridgeblog.org) (14 July 2023).

Barlau, Santiago. "Schools of Historical Interpretation and Their Characteristics." https://veintipico.com/schools-of-historical-interpretation-and … (17 Sep. 2023).

Deka, Meeta. "Folklore and Northeast Indian History." http://file.scirp.org/Html/7872.html (1 Aug. 2018).

Drapeau, Martin. "Subjectivity in Research: Why Not? But…" *TQR* 7Q/3 (9.1.2002).

Haokip, M. Thangkhosei. "The Impact of Christian Mission and British Colonialism among the Kuki People in Northeast India." http://kukiforum.com/2012/03/the-impact-of-christian-mission-and-british-colonialism-among-the-kuki-people-in-north-east-india/#_edn34 (13 Aug. 2018).

Hullfish, Steve. "Psychology of Color: Does a Specific Color Indicate a Specific Emotion?" http://provideocoalition.com/shullfish/story/psychology_of_color (6 Sep. 2023).

Kipgen, Paominlen. "Historiography, Definitions, Nature and Scope of History." https://www.academia.edu/31041228/

Historiography_Definitions_Nature_and_Scope_of_History (16 Apr. 2024).

Lane, Melissa. "Philosopher King." Encyclopedia Britannica. 28 Feb. 2023, https://www.britannica.com/topic/philosopher-king (5 Sep. 2023).

Little, Daniel. "Philosophy of History." The Stanford Encyclopedia of Philosophy. Winter 2020 ed. Edited by Edward N. Zalta. URL = https://plato.stanford.edu/archives/win2020/entries/history/ (5 Sep. 2023).

Mukharji, Aroop, Richard Zeckhauser. "Bound to Happen: Explanation Bias in Historical Analysis." *Journal of Applied History* 1(1), 2019, https://brill.com/view/journals/joah/joah-overview.xml (21 Sept. 2023).

Roediger, Henry L., K. Andrew DeSoto. "The Power of Collective Memory," https://www.scientificamerican.com/article/the-power-of-collective-memory/ (18 July 2023).

Serageldin, Ismail. "The Uses and Abuses of History." https://www.researchgate.net/publication/315700325_Uses_and_Abuses_of_history (17 Apr. 2024).

Mukharji, Aroop, Richard Zeckhauser. "Bound to Happen: Explanation Bias in Historical Analysis." *Journal of Applied History* 1(1), 2019. https://brill.com/view/journals/joah/joah-overview.xml (21 Sept. 2023).

Philips, Adam. "Similarities Between Secularism and Christianity," https://thewitness.org/similarities-between-secularism-and-Christianity/ (11 Apr. 2024).

Ryan, Eoghan. "Tertiary Sources Explained | Quick Guide & Examples."

Sawmpuia. "Positivist View of History." http://puchistory.blogspot.com/2015/01/positivist-view-of-history.html (31 July 2018).

Thomas, Linda E. "Womanist Theology, Epistemology, and a New Anthropological Paradigm," http://www.crosscurrents.org/thomas.htm (7 Oct. 2018).

Interview

Interview with Vanlalchhuanawma, former Principal of Aizawl Theological College, Aizawl and Union Biblical Seminary, Pune, 9th October, 2018.

Unpublished Materials

Hmingthanzuala, A. "Historiographical Tools of Church History Association of India: Problems and Prospects for the Twenty First Century History of Christianity in India." D.Th assessment paper, SATHRI, 2017.

Pachuau, Joy L. K. "Mizo Identity Bihchianna" ("A Closer Scrutiny of Mizo Identity"). A paper presented on a joint seminar organized at Synod Conference Centre, Aizawl by SCMI: Aizawl Theological College Unit on 20th January, 2018.

Vanlalchhuanawma. "The Main Issues in Modern Historiography." Unpublished paper.

Vanlalpeka. "*Quo Vadis* Tribal Christian Historiography? A Study on the Historiography of Vanlalchhuanawma." Unpublished paper.

Zhimomi, Kaholi. "Women during Armed Conflict: A Historical Re-reading of Indo-Naga Struggle in Nagaland from the Feminist Perspective." D.Th. dissertation, Senate of Serampore College, 2013.

Zoramthangi, Rosy. "Development of Methodological Trends in O.T. Study." D.Th. assessment paper, SATHRI, 2017.